D1389685

THE
POLITICAL
THEORY OF
AMERICAN
LOCAL
GOVERNMENT

STUDIES IN
POLITICAL
SCIENCE

THE POLITICAL THEORY OF AMERICAN LOCAL GOVERNMENT

Anwar Hussain Syed

UNIVERSITY OF MASSACHUSETTS

Random House • New York

To Shameem
my beloved

I am tempted to believe that what we call necessary institutions are often no more than institutions to which we have grown accustomed, and that in matters of social constitution the field of possibilities is much more extensive than men living in their various societies are ready to imagine.

Recollections of
Alexis de Tocqueville

Foreword

Many times in recent months friends and colleagues have asked me how I happened to write about the political theory of American local government. It all started one day several years ago when Dr. Alfred Williams, a member of the executive board of the Fels Institute of Local and State Government at the University of Pennsylvania, thought aloud to Dr. Stephen B. Sweeney, director of that Institute, that the changing concepts of sovereignty in the United States should be studied with special reference to local government. During my brief residence at the Fels Institute (1962–63), I undertook to explore the subject. But after some initial probing, I decided to make a study of the political theory of American local government in which concepts of sovereignty, being an important part of American political theory, would receive appropriate attention. The Fels Institute provided generous assistance in terms of typing help and a reduced teaching load for which I am grateful. However, they bear no responsibility for either the design and direction of the study or for my selection and interpretation of the material presented in it. While I should like to associate them with any merit that the book has, I alone am responsible for that which may be blameworthy.

I should like to express my gratitude to Professors Duane Lockard of Princeton University, Louis Hartz of Harvard University, William Andrews of Tufts University, Oliver Williams of the University of Pennsylvania, and John Harris and David Mayhew of the University of Massachusetts, for reading the entire manuscript and giving me the benefit of their comment. But once again the responsibility for what follows is mine. I must thank also Miss Anne Dyer Murphy and her associates at Random House for their editorial assistance.

My wife, Shameem Syed, also a political scientist, gave not only encouragement but also valuable counsel throughout the preparation of this book. Words will not express my gratitude to her.

A. H. S.

Amherst, Massachusetts
September 1, 1965.

Contents

THE
POLITICAL
THEORY OF
AMERICAN
LOCAL
GOVERNMENT

CHAPTER 1

Introduction

It is widely alleged that local government in the United States is unequal to the challenges confronting it. Its inadequacies are said to be many: apathy, inaction, organizational backwardness, legal and financial impotence, short-sightedness, parochialism, corruption, and the cardinal defect of excessive fragmentation. With the emergence of the metropolitan problem, reformers have urged municipal integration and consolidation, both of which have been slow in materializing. There are still far too many units of local government.

One reason suggested for the slow progress of reform is the nation's attachment to the Jeffersonian ideal of the "republic-in-miniature." Another is the failure of reformers to question the ethical status of this ideal. Certain writers criticize the reformers' overriding concern with programmatic efficiency and their relative indifference to questions of political value and virtue. Their functional approach has led to a mushrooming of special districts and authorities that quite often operate outside the political arena and become virtually free from popular control. Traditionally, the favorite slogan of many a reformer has been, "Take government out of politics!" According to Robert C. Wood:

> The premises on which the evaluation of urban governmental performance proceeded were more closely akin to those of public administration than to political theory. . . . The emphasis was not on a consideration of the capacity to govern, to provide orderly community existence, either in absolute power terms or in the legitimizing of that power. Rather it was oriented towards need. . . .
>
> Throughout the long years of wrestling with metropolitan problems, then, the norm of efficiency came to predominate. Issues associated with liberty and equality dropped out of sight when metropolitan governments were studied; issues concerned with welfare, in its narrow service sense, became the almost exclusive concern.[1]

There is merit in this criticism. Attention to political theory is not without advantage for understanding, especially reforming, political and governmental practice, for men are moved to action not only by their needs for services but also by their view of right and wrong, their images of the good society. If Jefferson was right in saying that sovereignty resides ultimately in the individual, that his personal supervision and direction of government constitute the height of democratic virtue, that the smaller the locality the more likely it is to be democratic, then why meddle with the existing organization of local government, why create "king-size" metropolitan governments? May it not be that the deficiencies of local government result from the machinations of corrupt politicians, the indifference of state legislatures, the lust for power of the federal government? Those who wish to change the status quo in local government ought to state their fundamental political values and assumptions. The experience may have an educative value for them as well as for their audience.

In recent years, several writers have explored the theoretical aspects of certain problems in American local government. Their endeavor, though conspicuous because of their declared concern with theory, is not novel. Jefferson formulated a theory of local government which remains a part of the American political folklore. In addition, for well over a century, judges, lawyers, public servants, politicians, reformers, and professors have been writing political theories of local government. Possibly, many of them did not intend to theorize and never realized that they had done so, but their innocence in this respect does not detract from the significance of their undertaking.

This book deals with the political theory of American local government—traditional and modern. Various schools of thought, debates, and opinions are identified and examined in the following pages. Here a broad line of distinction between them may be indicated. The traditional Jeffersonian theory asserts for localities a right to self-government as an expression of the sovereignty of the individual, derived from the doctrine of the sovereignty of the people, the individual's presumed condition in the state of nature, and a theory of natural rights. The inspiration of this theory was predominantly Lockean. In Alexis de Tocqueville it found a great elucidator, and it still has considerable popular appeal.

Nevertheless, its influence among serious students of local government would appear to have all but vanished. Other theories of local government have been advanced instead, covering a variety of fundamental issues: the nature of civil society and the individual's relation to it; the nature, especially with reference to divisibility, of sovereignty; the duty of government to render services of various kinds to the people; the nature of the American federal system. A common characteristic of these theories is that they ignore or reject concepts of natural rights and the social contract. Some of them are concerned with determining whether in a civil society a number of related but independent governments may exist at the same time, each having its own exclusive functional jurisdiction. Can governmental functions be divided between levels of government, or do they constitute a seamless web which does not admit of division?

These issues are recent in the context of local government, but they are old in American political theory, much of which, it will be recalled, relates to the nature of the Union. It may be appropriate to identify briefly the main currents of American thought on two subjects which figure importantly in theories of local government: the concept of the divisibility of sovereignty in a civil society, and the principle of aristocratic (or elitist) government as opposed to that of popular democracy. It will be seen that modern theorists of local government are applying to the study of their subject certain fundamental ideas which earlier American thinkers had developed in examining the issues of their times. They are still in the American tradition, even if they are not Jeffersonians.

First a word of caution about sovereignty. This term denotes and connotes matters that are as abstruse and complex as any in political thought. At the risk of oversimplification, we may say that sovereignty refers to the legal and/or actual supremacy of a center of governmental authority and power over all other centers of authority and power—governments, corporations, groups, individuals—within a given territory. As often it refers also to an authority's moral right to supremacy. Theorists of sovereignty have generally found the idea of absoluteness implicit in the idea of supremacy. Actually, absolutes are rare, if not altogether unavailable. Legal and moral statements about the location of sovereignty are not always accurately descriptive of the prevailing distribution and working of authority and power in society. It is not surprising, then, that several political thinkers and commentators—Benjamin Franklin, Philemon Bliss, Harold Laski, and the pluralists generally—have been wary of the concept of sovereignty. They would banish it from the field of political science. Not long ago, Jacques Maritain urged that "political philosophy must eliminate sovereignty both as a word and as a concept."[2]

However, it may be doubted that sovereignty, as a concept or as a slogan, will disappear from political debate. For long it has been a central theme in American thought on intergovernmental relations. Relating to supremacy, sovereignty is used as a slogan in the eternal struggles for power in society. In its legal and moral aspects, sovereignty is associated with legitimacy. Contenders for supremacy, however Machiavellian, will covet the title to legitimacy, because it will facilitate success and fortify it after they have achieved it. Even today certain American politicians find it useful to raise the banner of state sovereignty in resisting the federal government.

The authors of *The Federalist* insisted not only that sovereignty could be divided, but also that in the proposed Union it would be divided. The state governments would, Hamilton assured his readers, retain "certain exclusive and very important portions of sovereign power,"[3] indeed "all the rights of sovereignty which they before had, and which were not . . . *exclusively* delegated to the United States."[4] Later at the New York Convention he asserted that two "supreme powers" could exist together and even act in perfect harmony if their laws were addressed to different objects or to different parts of the same object. They were incompatible only when they were "aimed at each other or at one indivisible object."[5]* Madison likewise declared that the proposed constitution would leave to the states, which were "distinct and independent sovereigns," a "residuary and inviolable sovereignty" over all subjects not specifically granted to the Union.[6] He remained convinced that sovereignty could be divided. If it be indivisible, he wrote many years later, "the political system of the United States is a chimera." And again, "It is difficult to argue intelligibly concerning the compound system of government in the United States without admitting the divisibility of sovereignty."[7]

Madison and Hamilton had no doubt that governmental functions could be divided. The Union and the states would each have its own exclusive functional jurisdiction. But, interestingly enough, Hamilton thought that the line of functional division between the "general" and the state governments might change without violating the federal principle. The "extent" and "objects" of the federal authority were "mere matters of discretion." So long as the separate organization of the states existed by constitutional necessity, "though it should be in perfect subordination to the general authority of the union, it would still be, in fact and in theory . . . a confederacy."[8]

The theory of the divisibility of sovereignty found favor with a number of other American writers,[9] in addition to the United States Supreme Court.[10] In fact, the

---

* In the secrecy of the Philadelphia convention a few months earlier, Hamilton had expressed different ideas. He said: "The general power whatever be its form if it preserves itself, must swallow up the State powers, otherwise it will be swallowed up by them. . . . Two sovereignties cannot co-exist within the same limits." He thought that, if it were politically feasible, the states as such should be abolished. See Alpheus T. Mason, *Free Government in the Making* (New York: Oxford, 1956), pp. 201–202. Mason has given lengthy excerpts from Max Farrand's *The Records of the Federal Convention of 1787* (New Haven, 1911).

view generally prevailed in the eighteenth and early nineteenth centuries that sovereignty resided in the "people"
and not in governments.* The people could entrust
the exercise of their sovereignty partly to one government and partly to another. Governments were but
their agents. As *The Federalist* observed: "The federal
and State governments are in fact but different agents
and trustees of the people, constituted with different
powers and designed for different purposes."[11] Who
were the "people" under reference? Were they the people of America as a whole or were they the people of
the several states? *The Federalist* did not answer this
question specifically. Hamilton implied throughout the
papers that the sovereign people, of whom the proposed
federal government would be the creature, were the
people of America as a whole, as a nation. Madison
was inconsistent. In *The Federalist* No. 46, he wrote
that both the federal and the state governments would
be dependent upon the "great body of the citizens of
the United States." Addressing himself to those who

* The theory of popular sovereignty is clearly implicit in the
Declaration of Independence. It was also stated explicitly in
some early state declarations and constitutions. In the Massachusetts Proclamation of January 23, 1776, one reads: "It is a
maxim that in every Government there must exist, somewhere,
a supreme, sovereign, absolute and uncontrollable power; but
this power resides, always, in the body of the people, and it
never was, or can be delegated to one man or a few, the great
Creator having never given to men a right to vest others with
authority over them unlimited, either in duration or degree."
See Charles E. Merriam, *History of the Theory of Sovereignty*
(New York: Columbia University Press, 1900), pp. 159–160,
for this and other references to the prevalence of this doctrine.
In *The Rights of the British Colonies* (1764), James Otis
asserted that "an original supreme Sovereign, absolute, and uncontrollable, *earthly* power *must* exist in and preside over every
society . . . I say supreme absolute power is *originally* and
ultimately in the people." (Italics in original) Excerpted in
Mason, *op. cit.*, p. 95.

would not countenance a diminution of the power of the states, Madison, in *The Federalist* No. 45, asked:

> Was then the American Revolution effected . . . not that the people of America should enjoy peace, liberty, and safety, but that the governments of the individual States, that particular municipal establishments, might enjoy a certain extent of power and be arrayed with certain dignities and attributes of sovereignty?

If the sovereignty of the states could not be reconciled to the happiness of the people, their sovereignty must be sacrificed to the extent necessary, he added.

It is difficult to construe "the people of America" in these two statements to mean the "peoples of the states of America" as separate civil societies. In *The Federalist* No. 39, Madison also referred to the "people of America" who would ratify the proposed constitution. But here he specified that the "people of America" would act "not as individuals composing one entire nation, but as composing the distinct and independent States to which they respectively belong." This specification cannot fairly be said to apply to Madison's use of the phrase elsewhere in *The Federalist*.

As Charles Merriam notes,[12] it was the widely accepted theory of the sovereignty of the people that enabled political theorists and commentators to assert the divisibility of sovereignty and to pacify the rivalry between the states and the Union by referring constantly to their common superior, that uncertain entity, the people. But when the conflict between the nationalists and the particularists became acute, the identity of the sovereign people leaped out of obscurity. The nationalists asserted that the people were the same as the nation, the particularists that they were the peoples of the several states. Both sides discarded the notion that sovereignty could be divided.

The political theory of John C. Calhoun, which became the basis of Southern theories of Union-state relations, furthered the controversy. He started with the assumption, made before him by Bodin and Hobbes, that sovereignty was by nature indivisible; to divide it was to destroy it. "It is the supreme power in a state, and we might just as well speak of half a square, or half a triangle, as of half a sovereignty."[13] It was impossible to have a civil society consisting of half-sovereign states. The state must be either wholly and absolutely supreme or entirely subject. From these premises Calhoun argued that the American states were wholly sovereign and that the Union was merely an association of the states. Originally fully sovereign, the states did not surrender their sovereignty wholly upon entering the Union. They could not have surrendered it partially, even if they had wanted to do so, for it was impossible to do so. The federal government merely exercised certain powers of sovereignty delegated to it, but not ceded, by the states.* It should be mentioned that sovereignty, according to Calhoun, is not the sum of any number of given governmental powers, but instead a vital principle of the State from which all conceivable governmental powers issue and upon which they rest. Sovereignty is to a State as life is to the human body.

The theory of sovereignty developed by the nationalists is not far different from that of Calhoun. Francis Lieber, whose writings gave great impetus to the nationalist movement, regarded sovereignty as "the basis of all derived, vested or delegated powers, the source of all other political authority, itself without any source,

---

* John Taylor held a similar view. "In the creation of the federal government," he wrote, "the states exercised the highest act of sovereignty, and they may, if they please, repeat the proof of their sovereignty, by its [the federal government's] annihilation." See his *New Views of the Constitution of the United States* (Washington: Way and Gideon, Printer, 1823), p. 37.

imprescriptible in the nature of man."[14] A State cannot alienate its sovereignty any more than trees can
delegate the "right to sprout." Sovereign power may
not be unlimited or absolute; it is indivisible. According
to John Burgess, sovereignty is an indispensable mark
of statehood. It is the State's "original, absolute, unlimited, universal power over the individual subject and
over all associations of subjects."[15] Lieber and Burgess
both insist that it belongs to and resides in the nation.

The theory that sovereignty vested ultimately in the
individual received a blow from the advocates of states'
rights as well as the nationalists. Both rejected the contract theory. Calhoun maintained that the state of
nature, natural rights, and the social contract were all
hypothetical and fictitious. Government was a matter
of necessity, not of choice. "Like breathing, it is not
permitted to depend on our volition." According to
Lieber, sovereignty belongs to the civil society, having
"nothing whatsoever to do with the individual."[16] He
denied that the people were sovereign as a result of a
social contract. The very concept of the "people," he
thought, was inadequate. Distinguishing between the
"people" and the nation, he said the term "people" sig-
nified merely the aggregate of the inhabitants of a territory without any further "favorable" idea. The concept
of the nation, on the other hand, implied an "organic
unity" among a people having a common language, lit-
erature, institutions, the consciousness of a common
heritage, and a common destiny.[17]

The proposition that sovereignty vests in the corporate, organic community, or the nation, runs through
the writings of nationalist theorists. Jameson urges that
sovereignty resides in the body politic, "the corporate
unit resulting from the organization of many into one,
and not in the individuals constituting such unit, nor
in any number of them, as such, nor even in all of
them, except as organized into a body politic and acting

as such."[18] The sovereign community, or the nation, is a "living organism." Under the acknowledged influence of German philosophers such as Hegel, Stahl, and Bluntschli, Elisha Mulford regarded the nation as a "conscious," "moral" organism. Sovereignty was "the assertion of the self-determinate will of the organic people."[19] It should be noted that while the nationalist theorists did not all agree as to the role of the states within the American nation, they tended to conceive the Union as something transcending the individual, the states, and even the constitution. The nation would change its governmental system if and when it became obsolete. To the sovereign all things were possible.

John Burgess carried the theory of indivisible national sovereignty to its logical extreme. His argument is especially noteworthy in view of the marked similarity between his position and the view, urged by many contemporary students of local government, that functions of government constitute an indivisible "web," and that in reality there is in the United States only one government. Convinced that "for the present and the discernible future, the National State appears to be the organ for the interpretation, in last instance, of the order of life for its subjects," Burgess asserts that a federal State is an impossibility, a contradiction in terms.[20] What appears to be a federal State is in reality only a single State in which the constituent units have been accorded positions of prominence. Their powers do not add up to sovereignty or any portion of it. Indeed they are not States at all; they are merely organs of the government of the nation. The application of the term "State" to them is honorific, "without any corresponding substance."[21]

Writing in the *Political Science Quarterly,* Burgess challenged the "dogma" that the United States was an "indestructible union of indestructible states." Technological advances, national integration, and constitutional amendments had already made the states into "local governments containing, under the sovereignty of the Nation and the supremacy of the Nation's general representative, a large element of self-government."[22] The amended United States constitution enabled the national government to "nationalize" the whole of the private and public law of this country. Constitutional limitations of the state's power over local government indicated the "gradual dissolution of the commonwealth through the consolidation of the municipalities."[23] Burgess predicted that the legislative and judicial powers of the state would continue to gravitate towards the national government, their police powers towards the municipalities. The rapidly increasing power and influence of the modern city might well eventually push the state out of the American system of government.

> The two natural elements in our system are now the Community and the Nation. The former is the point of real local self-government; the latter that of general self-government; and in the adjustments of the future these are the forces which will carry with them the determining power. The commonwealth government is now but a sort of middle instance. Too large for local government, too small for general, it is beginning to be regarded as a meddlesome intruder in both spheres—the tool of the strongest interest, the oppressor of the individual. This has been its history in other lands and other times; and the mere fact that it professes to be popular here, while it has been princely or aristocratic elsewhere, will not save it from the same fate.[24]

A principle of elitist, aristocratic government is implicit in the concept of the corporate community. The welfare of this community is the primary concern of the State and its government. But even a majority of voters cannot claim a moral right to define conclusively the community's interest, for it transcends them, transcends even the entire populace. It is then no accident that theorists of the corporate community, like Edmund Burke, are also the proponents of aristocratic government, asserting that liberty and rights are creatures of the law. Calhoun thinks that liberty belongs to those who are fit to posses it, and Lieber and Burgess assert that the State is the source of all individual liberty. Burgess relates political liberty to political capacity. The Teutonic races, being especially endowed with political capacity, have the duty to undertake the civilization of mankind! Within the State, if it is composed of several ethnic groups, the Teutons should act as the guardians of the internal balance of power.[25] In this connection, his view of the ultimate end of the State is defined as the "perfection of humanity, the civilization of the world; the perfect development of the human reason and its attainment to universal command over individualism; the apotheosis of man."[26] The idea that the State should civilize the individual is apparent in Lieber's theory also. The State should do for man that which, though desirable, he cannot, will not or should not do alone.[27]

At the turn of the century, the nature of the Union was no longer the pervasive and consuming issue in political debate that it once was. But the movement away from the natural rights philosophy and its central figure, the individual, continued. The utilitarians were concerned with the determinable consequences of actions, using material success as their criterion of judgment. James Russell Lowell wondered if democracy was not by its nature doomed to a "dead level of commonplace." Charles Eliot Norton complained that far from promoting peace and civilization, democracy had placed political power in the hands of uncivilized men whose ignorance and lack of reason were beyond correction. The Godkin "liberals" became more interested in "purifying" democracy than in extending it. They pressed for civil service improvement, seeking the Benthamite objective of an honest, efficient and competent bureaucracy to administer the affairs of State. They advocated nonpartisanship in politics and strengthening of the executive power, with an item veto for the chief executive to restrain legislative "extravagance." The advent of Spencerian philosophy lent support to the proposition, already deduced from the "natural" laws of economics, that the path of progress was necessarily strewn with the bodies of the unfit. The "pauper" ought to be excluded from the ranks of the rulers. "On no sound political theory ought such a person to share in the political power of the State," wrote William Graham Sumner.

Even American "utopians" did not seek to restore the individual to his former "sovereign" position. Henry George and Edward Bellamy are concerned more with the corporate community than with the individual. Society is the source of all value, the repository of knowledge and culture from which succeeding generations of individuals benefit. Bellamy, who has no use for politics, argues that functions of the State are really administrative, requiring the services of technicians and functional experts. The position of socialist theorists, Laurence Gronlund and Daniel DeLeon, is similar, in that civil society, or the State, is represented as the "organic union of us all" to conquer the deficiencies of our "natural condition." Politics will be superfluous in the socialist good society. Only competent administrators, serving during good behavior, will be needed.

American pragmatism is also associated with a community emphasis rather than individualism. Both William James and John Dewey rejected "rationalistic" generalizations concerning human nature, natural law and rights, indeed any form of "natural determinism." The prevailing beliefs of society determined the rights of the individual and the limits of the government's powers and functions. Dewey emphasized the importance of developing "individuality," but asserted: "A stable recovery of individuality waits upon an elimination of the older economic and political individualism, an elimination which will liberate imagination and endeavor for the task of making corporate society contribute to the free culture of its members."[28]

Many conservative writers in this country have been elitist critics of individualism and democracy. Henry Adams had little faith in the modern man and none in democracy. Brooks Adams shared his brother's contempt for democracy and saw in the organization of a competent and centralized administration the only hope that civilization might survive. Paul Elmer More thought that the assumptions of Jeffersonian democracy, being false, could lead only to catastrophe. The governance of society was a function of the natural aristocracy. The end of individual and social endeavor was justice, which lay in the rule of reason over impulse. Irving Babbitt, an intellectual disciple of Burke, wrote his *Democracy and Leadership* (1924) to explain the principle of "veto power" which, like More's justice, meant the restraining check of conscience upon impulse. The doctrine of the rights of man, he thought, should give way to the principle of the "right man." Other critics of democracy like Ralph Adams Cram demanded that the nation eschew mediocrity and produce "men of character, capacity, and intelligence," placing such men, *"and such men only,* in all positions of power and responsibility."

Two other notable American political thinkers in this century have been highly critical of Jeffersonian theory. In Herbert Croly's first book, *The Promise of American Life* (1909), he reasoned that society is not a mechanical aggregation of separate individuals but a real entity of which individuals are a functional element. It moves ahead under the impact of historical tradition, not by natural law. The present is merely a bridge between the past and the future. The highest and the noblest form of society is the nation. Without national consciousness there can be no democracy, for democracy means more than the mere installation of certain institutions; it is the expression of the sovereign will of the nation toward the realization of a supreme ideal. Progress is a function of the top leadership; it does not result from the collective direction of all.

Finally, for forty years, Walter Lippmann has been urging that the "meddling" public be put in its proper place. In the Jeffersonian theory of natural rights and popular sovereignty he sees a Jacobin heresy and in its wide prevalence a principal cause of the decline of the West. He maintains that a plurality of voters has no right to determine the great issues of public policy for the corporate society, which, as Burke had said, is a partnership in virtue and a partnership between the living, the dead, and the unborn. In a liberal democracy, in the "traditions of civility," the people may elect their rulers, but they must not presume to instruct them. Governance is the prerogative of men who are civilized, who understand the traditions of their society and the moral order of the universe.[29]

Of course Jefferson has had his followers (among them John Taylor, William Leggett, Walt Whitman, Professor J. Allen Smith, and the populists), but there can be little doubt that most American political thinkers have tended to reject the important elements of his theory—natural rights, social contract, sovereignty of the individual, popular democracy. Considering, in addition to the foregoing survey, the predilections of the Founding Fathers, it would appear that a concept of the historic corporate community and a principle of aristocratic (or elitist) government dominate American political thought.

While we are not concerned in this book with the internal organization of local government, it may be mentioned in passing that the purposes and programs of municipal reformers in this country have had a distinctly elitist tendency. The advocates of at-large elections, non-partisanship, the merit system, the strong executive, the separation of administration from politics, the council-manager form of government, state administrative (instead of legislative) control of local government, were no Jacksonians. Edward C. Banfield and James Q. Wilson observe that many of them were "mugwumps," who "protested the transfer of power from the old public-serving elite to the new self-serving tycoons."[30] Their Anglo-Saxon, Protestant, upper- and upper-middle-class ethos had little use for contention and controversy. Permissible politics to them was a "disinterested effort to discover what is best for the community as a whole," not a struggle among partial and private interests.[31] The public interest, having been determined, should be served expeditiously and efficiently by technicians. Their reforms were intended, among other things, to handicap politically the "great unwashed"—the more recent immigrants and low status minority groups living on the other side of the tracks.[32]

On the one hand, it may be true, as Albert B. Hart wrote in 1907, that "the American no longer believes in the social compact. . . . The idea that government is an organism, that law has a force and a sanction not derived from previous consent, that the state is as old as society and not formed by society, seems to be unconsciously adopted as the basis of American government."[33] However, it is important to remember that the doctrines of natural rights and the social contract "continue to be articles of the popular creed,"[34] and still, to a considerable extent, sway popular thinking. The wide gulf between the intellectual and the common man creates a serious difficulty. If Jefferson's theory is poor, if it cannot be followed in practice, a widespread belief in its essential goodness and efficacy must engender cynicism among the people, hypocrisy among politicians, and disorderly thinking among planners and reformers.

CHAPTER 2

The Popular Theory

The tradition of local self-government in America has had experiential as well as ideological foundations. The two elements—political values, and actual experience with organizations of local government—have interacted upon and reinforced each other. Groups of early settlers in this country insisted that sovereignty ought to be diffused to the point of ultimate residence in the individual himself. The logic of their situation, which in some cases truly resembled a Lockean "state of nature," supported their view. They adopted certain governmental forms and rejected others according as these accommodated or repelled their fundamental assumptions in political philosophy. Thus, they gave their units of local government a considerable measure of autonomy. With the passage of time, the philosophy behind the practice of local autonomy acquired the status of a myth.

Cases will be found in early American history where bands of men came together and, without any external

authority, formed civil societies, some of which subsequently confederated into larger civil societies for specific purposes. They became the creators, rather than
the creatures, of what eventually became the states.
Such developments took place in New England, notably
in Rhode Island. Here the four original towns began as
four separate colonies before there was a state or
colony of Rhode Island. The town of Providence came
into being in 1636, Portsmouth (originally known as
Pocasset) in 1638, Newport in 1639, and Warwick in
1642–43.

Locke's description of the emergence of civil societies from the state of nature has a special ring of reality
when applied to the first towns of Rhode Island,* since
Providence, Portsmouth, and Newport each resulted
from a compact or compacts of association. Thirteen
men incorporated themselves as the town of Providence.[1] Another small group founded the town of
Portsmouth. Over a period of four months they made
two compacts, the first of which was signed by nineteen
men:

> We whose names are underwritten do here sol-
> emnly in the presence of Jehovah *incorporate* our-
> selves into a *Bodie Politick* and as he shall help,
> will submit our persons, lives and estates unto our
> Lord Jesus Christ, the king of kings and lord of
> lords and to all those perfect and most Absolute
> lawes of his given us in his holy word of truth,
> to be guided and judged thereby.

Perhaps considering that an acknowledgment of a
worldly connection should be added to their earlier expression of fidelity and subservience to Jehovah, twenty-

* Locke may have been aware of this. He once wrote: "Thus
in the beginning all the world was America." [Quoted in Louis
Hartz, *The Liberal Tradition in America* (New York: Harcourt,
Brace, 1955), p. 61.]

eight men signed a second compact some three months later.

> We, whose names are under (written doe acknowledge) ourselves the legal subjects of (his Majestie) King Charles, and in his name (doe hereby binde) ourzelves into a civill body politicke, unto his lawes according to matters of justice.[2]

On the day of the first compact, the nineteen signatories also elected a judge, agreeing to accord him all due honor "according to the lawes of God."

Subsequently, on February 28, 1639, nine men of Portsmouth decided to move from the original colony, forming a compact, while still at Portsmouth, to establish the new town of Newport. A year later, the residents of Portsmouth and Newport met together and formed a confederal government for the island of Aquidneck. They established the offices of governor, deputy governor, and four magistrates to be known as "assistants." The governor and two magistrates were to be chosen from one town; the deputy governor and two magistrates from the other. It should be noted that the confederating towns did not merge themselves into one. They entrusted the pursuit of their common objects to their confederal government, retaining individually the management of local affairs. Their compact for the union provided that "each Towne shall have the Transaction of the affaires that shall fall within their own Towne." Not only did they contribute equally to the confederal treasury from which their common expenses were defrayed, but each also carried the responsibility for assessing and collecting confederal as well as local taxes.

In 1641 the General Court of Elections for Aquidneck decided that the "state" acquire a manual seal with a sheaf of arrows engraved upon it, bearing the motto: *Amor vincet omnia.* Apparently this was the first time in American history that a civil society referred to itself as a "state." That it adopted a seal was also significant, for the possession of a seal had traditionally been regarded as an insignia of sovereignty. In May, 1647, the freemen of Providence, Portsmouth, Newport, and Warwick met at Portsmouth to accept a parliamentary charter that Roger Williams had brought for them from England. At the same time, they constituted a government for the united colony, which later became the state of Rhode Island.* Next year Providence requested the General Assembly of the new colony to grant it a charter of incorporation. The Assembly granted it

> *a free and absolute charter of civil incorporation and government* . . . together *with full power and authority to govern and rule themselves* . . . by such a form of civil government as by voluntary consent of all, or the greater part of them, shall be found most suitable unto their state and condition: and to that end, to make and ordain such civil orders and constitutions . . . so to place and displace officers of justice as they or the greater part of them shall, by one consent, agree unto. Provided nevertheless, that the said laws . . . be *conformable to the laws of England, so far as the na-*

* This union was disrupted in 1651, when William Coddington procured from the Council of State a charter authorizing him to rule Rhode Island autocratically for life. But the towns secured a repeal of Coddington's charter in 1653 and effected their re-union in 1654. A general assembly, consisting of six representatives from each town, met at Warwick and signed the compact of re-union. Coddington, it may be of interest to note, was an ambitious and restless person. He was the first judge in Portsmouth (1638–39), the first judge in Newport (1639–40), and the first governor of the union of these two towns. He would appear also to have been the moving spirit behind the establishment of these towns and their union.

ture and constitution of the place will admit, yet
always reserving to the aforesaid General Assembly power and authority so to dispose the
general government of that plantation as it stands
in reference to the rest of the plantations as they
shall conceive, from time to time, most conducing
to the general good of the said plantation.[3]
(*Italics supplied*)

It will be seen that the General Assembly gave Providence a sweeping "home rule" charter. It fashioned a
relationship between the town and the colony patterned
after the relationship that was understood to exist between the colony and the Crown. The laws of the
colony itself must conform to the laws of England only
"so near as the nature and constitution of the place
will admit." There is no requirement yet that the laws
of Providence must conform also to the laws of the
colony. For at this time Providence, together with the
other three towns, had the right to annul such colonial
laws as did not suit its "nature and constitution." The
colony reserved to itself only that part of the government of Providence "as it stands in reference to the rest
of the plantations." The Crown possessed a similar
power over Rhode Island. Legally, Providence was not
yet a vassal of the colonial government.

For many years, the towns of Rhode Island possessed
the right to initiate, and annul, general colonial legislation. Under a law of 1647, matters of general concern
to the colony could be raised first in the towns themselves. The initiating town would discuss and debate
the question in its town meeting and then communicate
the majority decision to the other three towns. The latter would similarly "agitate" the matter and conclude
it by majority vote. The clerk of each town would then
send the vote to the General Court, a committee of the
General Assembly having the authority to legislate be-

tween the Assembly sessions. If a majority opinion on the issue resulted from these votes, the General Court declared it to be the law of the land until the next session of the General Assembly. Any laws that the General Court made on its own initiative had only a provisional status. They must be submitted to the towns for their approval. Furthermore, the towns could annul a law of the General Court if any part of it happened to be unsuitable to "the constitution of the place." This right of the towns of Rhode Island remained substantially in force until 1664.

Four towns in New Hampshire—Exeter, Dover, Portsmouth, and Hampton—also resulted from self-originating compacts. In 1639 the settlers of Exeter entered into the following compact, drafted for them by their minister and leader, John Wheelright, a brother-in-law of the celebrated Mistress Anne Hutchinson:

> Wee . . . brethren of the church of Exeter . . . considering with ourselves the holy will of God and our owne necessity that we should not live without wholesome lawes & civil government among us, of which we are altogether distitute, doe . . . combine ourselves together to erect and set up amongst us such government as shall be to our best discerning, agreeable to the will of god . . . (and) to such godly & christian lawes as are established in the Realme of England to our best knowledge, & to all other lawes w^h shall upon good grounds be made and inacted amongst us. . . .
> *Mon—5th, d. 4th 1639.*[4]

It was not without reason then that at the bicentennial celebrations of Exeter, a citizen, referring to this compact, boasted: "It is the only act of incorporation our town has ever had. We are a self-created body politic."[5]

Independent and self–governing, the other three towns of New Hampshire also created their own governments. Their subsequent union made the state of New Hampshire, the state did not create them.[6] There is some evidence to suggest that Massachusetts also, far from being the original creator of its towns, emerged as a civil society from their union.[7]

The claim that the right to local self-government is founded in American history is then not without foundation. The experience of New England may not have had many parallels elsewhere, but it did become the ideal in local government which other parts of the country might approximate. The spirit of local autonomy, however, was not confined to the states of New England. From time to time until the middle of the nineteenth century, New Yorkers amended their charter as they saw fit, acting through charter commissions whose members they elected. No state law, relative to their affairs, could take effect until the City approved it.[8]

In its passage towards the status of an ideology, the principle of local autonomy received inestimable support from Alexis de Tocqueville. His celebrated work, *Democracy in America,* contains a classic exposition of the theory and practice of local self-government in the United States. But although some of his observations have become proverbial, others, equally significant, may not be well known.

Tocqueville begins his description of American government and politics by saying that "whenever the political laws of the United States are to be discussed, it is with the doctrine of the sovereignty of the people that we must begin."[9] Even during the colonial period this doctrine dominated local government and politics, ruling "secretly in the provincial assemblies, and especially in the townships." By the time of his visit, it had fully matured and become the governing principle of the American polity, having acquired "all the practical development that the imagination can conceive." The modes of its expression might vary, of course, depending upon time and circumstance. Sometimes the people, acting personally and directly, made laws as the Athenians once did. On other occasions, their representatives transacted the law-making business in their name and under their supervision.[10] Tocqueville observed that the doctrine of the sovereignty of the people actually denoted the sovereignty of the individual.

> In the nations by which the sovereignty of the people is recognized, every individual has an equal share of power and participates equally in the government of the state. . . . Every individual is always supposed to be as well-informed, as virtuous, and as strong as any of his fellow citizens. He obeys society . . . *because he acknowledges the utility of an association of his fellow men* and he knows that no such association can exist without a regulating force. . . . This doctrine is universally admitted in the United States.[11]

The individual's sovereignty meant his equality with all other individuals with respect to moral status, intelligence, political rights and power.

Tocqueville found that in its relation to the state, the township, as a corporation, was sovereign like any individual. Its independence was a "natural consequence of this very principle of the sovereignty of the people." In varying degrees, all American states recognized the principle of local independence, but it had blossomed the fullest in New England. It was here, in the townships, said Tocqueville, that political life had first started in America. One might even say that originally each one of them began as an independent nation. "They did not receive their powers from the central authority, but, on the contrary, *they gave up a portion of their independence to the state. This is an important distinction and one that the reader must constantly recollect.*"[12] (Italics supplied) He noted that even though the townships were no longer wholly independent, they were subordinate to the state only in matters that were state-wide in scope. In their local concerns they were still free. "Among the inhabitants of New England I believe that not a man is to be found who would acknowledge that the state has any right to interfere in their town affairs."[13] These towns conducted their own affairs; they bought and sold, sued and were sued, increased or decreased their budgets without intervention from an outside authority. It was true that in certain cases the township had to report its actions to the state government, but the latter had no field agents to oversee, direct or punish the local government. The elected local officials could not be "cashiered or promoted" by the state government.

The independence and authority of local government in New England were the objects of universal interest and admiration. Significantly, Tocqueville observed that men turned their loyalties towards an active center of power. The citizen of a New England township loved and honored it not merely because he was born there. He did so because "it is a free and strong community, of which he is a member, and which deserves the care spent in managing it. . . . Without power and independence a town may contain good subjects, but it can have no active citizens."[14] It was unfortunate that European nations had not experienced the advantages of local autonomy, because municipal institutions added to the strength of free nations. "Town meetings are to liberty what primary schools are to science; they bring it within the people's reach, they teach men how to use and how to enjoy it. A nation may establish a free government, but without municipal institutions it cannot have the spirit of liberty."[15] Tocqueville rejected the argument that a central government would administer the affairs of each locality better than could its own citizens. This assertion might hold where the central power was active, alert, and enlightened, while the local authorities were ignorant, slow, and passive. He warned that centralization might well aggravate any sluggishness and incapacity that happened to characterize the citizenry. At any rate, it was out of place where "the people are as enlightened, as awake to their interests, and as accustomed to reflect on them as the Americans are."[16] Even where the people did not possess the "passions and knowledge" to look after their own affairs, decentralization should be recommended, for a central government, however skillful and enlightened, could not "of itself embrace all the details of the life of a great nation. Such vigilance exceeds the powers of man."[17]

A centralized government cannot do much more than maintain internal peace. It will excel in routinizing and standardizing its *modus operandi,* creating that "drowsy regularity in the conduct of affairs which the heads of the administration are wont to call good order and public tranquility; in short, it excels in prevention, but not in action."[18] When it needs popular support, it asks the people to follow its instructions without knowing the *raison d'etre* or the guiding principles of the enterprise itself. These, observed Tocqueville, "are not the conditions on which the alliance of the human will is to be obtained." The individual must be free and he must be responsible for his actions. In the absence of self-determination, he would rather remain a *"passive spectator"* than be a *"dependent actor."*

The conduct of American local self-government was not without its dark side, however. Occasionally, one would find cases of gross apathy and neglect, even "disgraceful blemishes." In America, as elsewhere, popular interest in government was spasmodic. Consequently, public undertakings which required continuous and careful attention over an extended period of time were abandoned or neglected. But, on balance, Americans

gave more of their time, effort and interest in promoting
the public good than did the people of any other country in the world. To Alexis de Tocqueville, it was clear
that the American system of decentralized government
was preferable to any other.

> It profits me but little, after all, that a vigilant
> authority always protects the tranquility of my
> pleasures and constantly averts all dangers from
> my path, without my care or concern, if this same
> authority is the absolute master of my liberty and
> my life, and *if it so monopolizes movement and
> life that when it languishes everything languishes
> around it, and when it sleeps everything must sleep,
> and then when it dies the state itself must perish.*[19]
> (Italics supplied)

Local autonomy was essential even to maintaining
national cohesion and security. If the laws freed the
human spirit and, by engaging the individual in the
business of governance, joined his loyalty to the nation
with his interests, "thoughts and habits of life," patriotism would be "consolidated into a durable and rational
sentiment." A democracy without autonomous local government would not resist the forces of despotism. A
people that had not learned to use freedom in small
concerns would not know how to use it in great affairs
of the State. "Those who dread the violence of the mob
and those who fear absolute power ought alike to desire
the gradual development of provincial liberties."[20] Tocqueville reported that Americans of his time understood
well the vital importance of local autonomy to their liberty and democracy.*

---

* De Tocqueville notes that he found no one in America, or
for that matter in England, who did not regard local autonomy
as a great good. "I heard citizens attribute the power and pros-
perity of their country to a multitude of reasons, but they all
placed the advantages of local institutions in the foremost rank."
Ibid., p. 96.

In explaining the origin of local government Tocqueville had many keen insights. The village or a township, he wrote, is the only perfectly natural association, constituting itself wherever a number of people come together. "It is man who makes monarchies and establishes republics, but the township seems to come directly from the hand of God."[21] It must be added that Tocqueville did not see divinity in the locality, as indeed some churchmen are said to do.[22] The township, he said, is rooted in the "coarser material" of human nature. It is "secretly self-produced in the midst of a semi-barbarous society." With the advance of civilization, local autonomy may become difficult to maintain. "A highly civilized community can hardly tolerate a local independence, is disgusted at its numerous blunders, and is apt to despair of success before the experiment is completed."[23] Localities will not be able to defend their "immunities" against a possessive central authority unless their freedom is firmly embedded in the mores of the society. "Thus until the independence of townships is amalgamated with the manners of a people, it is easily destroyed; and it is only after a long existence in the laws that it can be thus amalgamated."[24]

Would the habit of local self-government endure in America? Tocqueville was not certain. He inclined to the view that the greatest danger to self-government arose from the very principle upon which its practice in the United States was based, namely, the principle of the sovereignty of the people and of the individual.

That the people may be absolutely and uncontrollably sovereign, that they may do any and all things, is, according to Tocqueville, "an impious and detestable maxim." The people have no right to violate a general law, "which bears the name of justice," and which has been made and sanctioned by mankind. They must exercise their authority in subordination to the "sovereignty of mankind." Those who assert that the people

can never be unreasonable and unjust in the conduct
of their own affairs are flatterers; they speak the language of slaves.[25]

In America, as in other democracies, the majority
exercised the sovereignty of the people. It established
a legal despotism in the legislature. It made government
officials into its passive agents, treating them "as a
master does his servants." Sometimes it encouraged
them to exceed their legal authority and do things that
would astonish even those who were accustomed to
arbitrary rule. Thus "habits are formed in the heart of
a free country which may some day prove fatal to its
liberties."[26]

Armed with overwhelming authority, the majority
overawed dissidents into silence. Once it had spoken all
controversy must cease. "I know of no country in which
there is so little independence of mind and real freedom
of discussion as in America."[27] The majority prescribed
the outer limits of disagreement; woe to him who
should dare cross them. While it did not take away his
life or his property or even his freedom to move about,
it inflicted upon him a severer punishment, declaring:

> You are free to think differently from me and to
> retain your life, your property . . . but you are
> henceforth a stranger among your people. You
> may retain your civil rights, but they will be use-
> less to you. . . . . Your fellow creatures will shun
> you like an impure being; and even those who
> believe in your innocence will abandon you, lest
> they should be shunned in their turn.[28]

The list of democratic excesses continued. Under fire
from the sovereign people, representative government
was departing from the American scene. Voters instructed their representatives to follow given courses of
action. Public and private affairs tended to merge into
one another. Sovereign authority being accessible to all,

it was easily exploited by men "who speculate upon its weakness and live upon ministering to its passions."

Tocqueville maintained that the doctrine of the sovereignty of the individual was also subversive of liberty. We have seen that he construed the individual's sovereignty to mean his equality with other individuals. In America the equality of all men in the sight of God and before law had been supplemented by an equality of condition. A considerable leveling of wealth had taken place. Primary education was open to all. Higher education was desired by only a few. Americans had cultivated a passion for equality. It put its stamp upon their politics, government and laws. It molded the attitudes of rulers and the habits of the governed. In the opening paragraph of his book, Tocqueville wrote: "The more I advanced in the study of American society, the more I perceived that this equality of condition is the fundamental fact from which all others seem to be derived and the central point at which all my observations constantly terminated."[29]

In a state of equality, such as that Tocqueville professedly witnessed here, citizens bear no traditional ties to one another. None is obliged to do the bidding of another. Equality in a democracy brings the "kindred more closely together, while it throws citizens more apart."[30] Engaged in the pursuit of his own welfare, each man lives in his own little world, consisting of his immediate family and close friends. Living apart from others, he is unconcerned with their fate. The sovereign individual, equal of all, lives in himself and for himself. This disposition, known to doctrine as individualism, subverts the virtues of public as well as personal life.

> In ages of equality every man seeks for his opinions within himself . . . [and] all his feelings are turned towards himself alone. . . .
> Selfishness blights the germ of all virtue; indi-

vidualism, at first, only saps the virtues of public life; but in the long run it attacks and destroys all others . . . individualism is of democratic origin, and it threatens to spread in the same ratio as the equality of condition.[31]

Individualism endangers liberty in two ways. The individual, engrossed in his private affairs, is often unwilling to devote interest, time and effort to discharging the duties of self-government. He regards these duties —participating in elections, attending meetings, rendering personal service in support of the government—as "idle amusements." If his continued enjoyment of equality becomes uncertain, he is liable to surrender his liberty to a paternalistic government and require it to maintain his equality of condition with others. The passion of democratic men for equality is "ardent, insatiable, incessant, invincible; they call for equality in freedom; and if they cannot obtain that, they still call for equality in slavery."[32] Later in his book, Tocqueville writes:

As in periods of equality no man is compelled to lend his assistance to his fellow men, and none has any right to expect much support from them, everyone is at once independent and powerless. . . . His independence fills him with self-reliance and pride among his equals; his debility makes him feel from time to time the want of some outward assistance, which he cannot expect from any of them, because they are all impotent and unsympathizing. In this predicament he naturally turns his eyes to that imposing power which alone rises above the level of universal depression [i.e. the State].[33]

The vice of apathy might be overcome, and equality made compatible with liberty, if men could always live in a state of abundance. This, however, cannot be. No technology can keep pace with man's passion for well-being which, like the Hobbesian desire for power, knows no bounds and can never be satiated. Democratic man must moderate his desire. Will he? On the whole, Tocqueville is pessimistic. About the American democrat he is equivocal. Americans did participate in public affairs; not out of a philosophical or doctrinal persuasion,* but from the expectation that a government in which they participated would let them "acquire the things they covet" and ensure them peaceful enjoyment of their possessions.[34] They were possessed of a ceaseless, tormenting desire for material goods, in a hurry to possess the things that lay within reach and worried about a thousand others that might elude them.[35] However, he wrote also that although the Americans' desire for physical gratification was "vehement," it was not indiscriminate; "reason, though unable to restrain it, still directs its course."[36]

Anticipating certain modern writers who have spoken of lonely crowds and of escapes from freedom, Tocqueville observed that as the equality of condition materialized among a people, society gained in importance at the expense of the individual.

> Every citizen, being assimilated to all the rest, is lost in the crowd, and nothing stands conspicuous but the great and imposing image of the people at large. This naturally gives the men of democratic periods a lofty opinion of the privileges of society. . . . They are willing to acknowledge that the power which represents the community has far more information and wisdom than any of the members of that community; and that it is the duty, as well as the right, of that power to guide as well as govern each private citizen.[37]

---

* In America, he writes, "hardly anybody talks of the beauty of virtue, but they maintain that virtue is useful and prove it every day." *Ibid.,* II, p. 121.

The paternalism resulting from a relentless pursuit of equality need not take the form of old-fashioned tyranny. It may well endeavor to serve the people and make them "happy"; supply their needs, guide their "industry," facilitate their pleasures, provide them a sense of security; indeed "spare them all the care of thinking and all the trouble of living."[38] This type of a mild despotism might easily be combined with some superficial outward symbols of freedom. "It might even establish itself under the wing of the sovereignty of the people."[39]

Tocqueville's tribute to the New England township and the principles underlying it should be read along with his reservations noted above. Some interesting points emerge from his position. He is concerned with showing how a particular social condition will bring about a certain political system.[40] The principle of the sovereignty of the individual, underlying the system of local self-government he described, was an operative principle, representing an actual state of affairs—equality of condition. In other words, this system of government was the product of a certain stage in the march of history. What would happen to it when equality no longer prevailed and when, consequently, the individual's sovereignty, instead of being actual, reverted to its more usual status of a theoretical assumption? Quite likely it would give way to another system. Men, at once covetous and impotent, might resort to a governmental order that would use its coercive power to recreate equality.

But even while equality prevailed, government would suffer from serious defects. Citizens would tend naturally to neglect it. Designing men would exploit its weakness to their own advantage. The notion that they were sovereign would assure men that they were always right. This would make them intolerant of dissident minorities. Government calls for cooperation among individuals, but in the theory under review, the incentives to cooperation are internal and by no means compelling. The radical vice of this theory is that it confers sovereignty upon the impotent.

The popular American theory of local self-government that Tocqueville described derives its major assumptions and premises from Thomas Jefferson, the first, and also the foremost, advocate of local self-government. Jefferson would divide the counties into "wards" of five or six square miles each. Such a ward would become a "little republic," exercising self-government in all those matters which it was best qualified to handle. These according to Jefferson were: care of the poor, roads, police, administration of justice in minor cases, and elementary exercises for the militia. This list might be enlarged, the guiding principle being that the wards should govern "all those concerns which, being under their eye, they would better manage than the large republics of the county or state."[41] Jefferson went on to invest his wards with another significant role. Their existence, he thought, would enable even the distant state government to function as a direct democracy. Matters of statewide concern might be submitted to the wards for consideration by the people. On an appointed day, all wardens in the state would call their respective citizens to meet and deliberate the questions referred to them. Thus, on any given subject, a genuine sense of the people throughout the state would emerge on a single day. The state government would be guided accordingly. This procedure "would enable the state to act in mass, as your people have so often done, and with so much effect by their town meetings,"[42] he wrote to John Adams in 1813.

Three years later, we find Jefferson concerned about the unrepresentative character of certain organs of government in the country. He was also disturbed about the inefficient and irregular administration of government in the counties. "Follow the principle," he told

Samuel Kercheval in a letter of July 12, 1816, "and the knot unties itself." By "principle," Jefferson meant:

> In government, as well as in every other business of life, it is by division and sub-division of duties alone, that all matters, great and small, can be managed to perfection. . . . And the whole is cemented by giving to every citizen, personally, a part in the administration of the public affairs.[43]

Once again he proposed the division of the counties into wards. This time he settled the question of size by laying down the criterion that a ward should be small enough so that every citizen could attend its meetings and "act in person." The people of each ward should have authority to dispose of all matters "relating to themselves exclusively." To the list he had earlier given to Adams he now added: education; election of judges and constables; election or selection of jurors; submission to appropriate authorities of election returns from the ward for elective office in other governments; election, and presumably also the maintenance, of a "military company." The justices chosen in the wards would together constitute the county court. In addition to their normal judicial work, they would administer all such affairs as might concern the whole county. The proposed plan of governmental decentralization would, Jefferson thought, have a two-fold consequence. By involving every citizen actively and personally in the conduct of his government, it would strengthen his devotion to republicanism and to the independence of his country. Secondly, the government of the county would become superfluous, having been relieved "of nearly all its business." Jefferson then paid the New England township the compliment that has since often been quoted: "These wards, called townships in New England, are the vital principles of their governments, and have proved themselves the wisest invention ever devised by the wit of man for the perfect exercise of self-government, and for its preservation."[44]

Jefferson thought that there ought to be four centers of republican government in the country: the general federal republic for all foreign and federal concerns; the state republics for matters which relate to the citizens of each state exclusively; the county republics for the duties and concerns of the county; and "the ward republics, for the small, and yet numerous and interesting concerns of the neighborhood." A careful examination of Jefferson's four-tier scheme would reveal that it admitted of only one really active and vital center of government, namely, the "ward republics." The state governments were far from being active in those days, and the functions of the county were to be transferred to the wards. Jefferson had a similar fate in store for the federal government. According to him, the appropriate sphere of federal concern included only foreign affairs and defense. In connection with defense, Jefferson did not favor the maintenance of a standing army, for it would "overawe the public sentiment." The militia, which would receive its elementary exercises in the ward republics, would supply the nation's first response to a foreign invasion if and when it came. Nor would he suffer a navy of any considerable proportion, for that, by its expenses and by the wars in which it would implicate the people, "would grind us." The defense establishment of the federal government was thus eliminated. Of political relations with foreign nations the United States ought to have none. "I am for free commerce with all nations," Jefferson once told Elbridge Gerry, "political connection with none; and little or no diplomatic establishment."[45] There was no need for this country to make treaties and reestablish connections with the nations of Europe—"that field of slaughter!" Finally, as regards commercial relations, the federal government should not meddle with them at all.

Let the General Government be reduced to foreign concerns only, and let our affairs be disentangled from those of all other nations, except as to commerce, *which the merchants will manage the better, the more they are left free to manage for themselves,* and our general government may be reduced to a very simple organization, and a very unexpensive one; a few plain duties to be performed by a few servants.[46] (Italics supplied)

In short the "federal republic" and the "county republics" were to have little, if anything, to do.

Although it is true that Jefferson was a fierce advocate of the states' rights, his concern was really with their *relative* power. He was interested not so much in strengthening the state governments as in weakening the federal government. In his letter to Gerry quoted above, he announced: "I am for preserving to the states the powers not yielded up by them to the Union."[47] In his First Inaugural Address, he complimented the states as "the most competent administrations for our domestic concerns and the *surest bulwarks against anti-republican tendencies.*" (Italics supplied) Here again he was preoccupied with containing "anti-republican tendencies," that is to say, with preventing the concentration of power in the federal government. Note also that the states were "competent" for administering domestic concerns from the standpoint of constitutional right, not from that of capacity. In the same address, Jefferson also defined the "sum of good government." A government should "restrain men from injuring one another, [and should] leave them otherwise free to regulate their own pursuits of industry and improvement."[48]

Jefferson's definition of republicanism is significant. It implies, he wrote to John Taylor on May 28, 1816, a government by the citizens in mass, "acting directly and personally." A government is more or less republican according as it has more or less of this "ingredient of the direct action of the citizens."[49] A perfect republic can materialize only in a small jurisdiction such as a New England township. Where direct and personal citizen participation in government cannot obtain, resort must be made to representatives. But a representative is no more than an agent of his constituents, their spokesman. They have the right to give him instructions concerning his conduct in government that he must obey.[50] A representative assembly is only a congress of ambassadors representing the sovereign constituents.

In a letter to Francis Gilmer dated June 7, 1816, Jefferson restated—this time more clearly and emphatically—his view of the role of a representative. The true office of a legislator, he wrote, "is only to declare and enforce our natural rights and duties, and to take none of them away from us."[51] The "natural duty" of an individual amounted only to respecting the natural rights of other individuals. Accordingly, the laws ought to do no more than restrain individuals from invading the natural rights of one another. Jefferson declared: "The idea is quite unfounded that upon entering society we give up any natural rights."[52]

The individual is still sovereign. The state of nature still prevails except in one respect: the individual has resigned his right to judge and punish violations of the law of nature by other individuals. He accepts the community as the umpire. But even so, the function of the umpire should, as far as possible, be performed in the smallest possible community, the ward republic, where performance will take place under the watchful eye of the individual himself.

The idea of the sovereignty of the individual receives further support from Jefferson in a letter to Samuel Kercheval written on July 12, 1816. Following Locke,

Jefferson observed that each individual should participate in framing the constitutional compact under
which he would live; the action of his forefathers in this
respect not being far-reaching enough. A constitution
should be revised at stated intervals. Laws and institutions should benefit from the progress of the human
mind. A civilized people ought not to remain "ever
under the regimen of their barbarous ancestors." Since
every twenty years or so, a new generation, a new
majority, emerged in society, a constitution should last
no longer.

> Each generation is as independent as the one pre-
> ceding, as that was of all which had gone before.
> It has then, like them, a right to choose for itself
> the form of government it believes most promotive
> of its own happiness . . . and it is for the peace
> and good of mankind, that a solemn opportunity
> of doing this every nineteen or twenty years, should
> be provided by the constitution. . . .[53]

Jefferson rejects disdainfuly the concept of the historic, corporate community. Upon the consideration of
the present generation its "barbarous ancestors" can
make no claims. "The dead have no rights!" Do the
unborn have any rights? In his denunciations of the
public debt, Jefferson denies that the present has any
claims upon the future. But does the present generation
bear any responsibility to the coming generations? One
wonders how Jefferson would have answered these
questions. And were he to answer them in the affirmative, how would he do so without conceding the existence of the corporate community?

It should be noted that Jefferson's advocacy of the
ward republics is indissolubly connected with small
rural communities. The wards were to be small enough
so that every citizen could attend the town meeting and
"act in person." It is doubtful that Jefferson would sup-

port the government of large cities, whose "mobs" "add just so much to the support of pure government, as sores do to the strength of the human body." The smallness of jurisdictional size and the rural setting were vital to the successful practice of republicanism. For "it is the manners and spirit of a people which preserve a republic in vigour," and of the "manners and spirit" that conduced republican vigor God had given the farmer generously.[54]

Although support for Jefferson's theory of sovereignty may be found in the writings of several Western political philosophers, the fountain from which the mainstream of American tradition in this respect issues is John Locke's second essay on civil government.[55] Locke does not address himself specifically to the individual's right to join with others in forming lesser governmental associations, such as a local government, but the existence of such a right can be deduced from his view of the nature of civil society* and the individual's relation to it.

In order to understand the "original" of political power, says Locke, we must repair to the state of nature. There men live in a state of perfect equality and perfect freedom. They are subject to no restraints except those of the law of nature, which is the law of divine reason. Each man fashions his behavior according to his own light, "without asking leave, or depending upon the will of any other man." There are no magistrates to enforce the law of nature. Each individual is entitled, as well as any other, to punish the offender.[56] When, in order to do away with the inconveniences of the state of nature, the individual, joined with other individuals, establishes a civil society, he sur-

---

* Locke often uses the terms "civil society," "political society," "community," "civil government," "government" synonymously. Rarely does he distinguish between society and government.

renders to it his "natural power" to judge and punish violations of the law of nature.[57] All private individual judgments cease, and the community becomes the umpire. Its powers are exercised by the government it constitutes. It should be noted that the individual's surrender of sovereignty is partial and provisional. The power of government is fiduciary, granted for the pursuit of certain specific ends. The "people" retain the "supreme power to remove or alter the legislative" if they find its acts to be violative of the trust placed with it.[58]

How do civil societies come into being? Repeatedly, Locke asserts that "any number of men" may form a civil society and resign unto it their individual "executive" power. Others in the state of nature may join subsequently and "incorporate" with the society already made.[59] Considering that most men are born under one government or another, can a number of men unite to form a new government? Locke answers this question in the affirmative, saying that any person "born under the dominion of another has a right to become the ruler or subject of another government."[60] He rejects the argument that the original authors of the civil society resigned the rights and privileges of the state of nature not only on their own behalf but also on that of their posterity. In surrendering their natural liberty, our forefathers committed only themselves. A child is born free, says Locke, and in full possession of man's rights in the state of nature. He is subject of no country or government. "Nothing can make any man so [subject or member of a commonwealth], but his actually entering into it by positive engagement, and express promise and compact."[61]

The above propositions in Locke's essay on civil government lend support to the doctrine of the sovereignty of the individual. Yet Locke would probably not endorse the view that the individual has a right to participate personally and directly in the conduct of government. The individual had two powers in the state of nature: the power to promote his own preservation and that of mankind; and the power to punish violations of the law of nature. The first power "he gives up to be regulated by laws made by the society," and "the power of punishing he wholly gives up."[62] The main function of the civil society is judicial in character, to be performed by "indifferent" judges according to standing rules that are "indifferent and same to all parties." The individual cannot appropriately participate in the settlement of issues where his personal interests are at stake. It should be recalled that the state of nature was not to be endured because of the "evils which necessarily follow from men's being judges in their own cases." And again, "it is easy to be imagined that he who was so unjust as to do his brother an injury will scarce be so just as to condemn himself for it."[63] Thus a distinction ought to be made between the individual's rights and his powers in the state of nature. Locke might agree with Jefferson that upon entering civil society we give up none of our rights. But he would reject the position, to which Jefferson tends, that we do not give up any of our powers either.

In advocating direct democracy, Jefferson necessarily assumes that the individual, merely by virtue of being human, understands the law of nature. Locke, on the other hand, observes that the individual, while capable potentially of understanding the law of nature, must be a "studier" of that law in order actually to understand it. Furthermore, in applying this law to specific situations, he must not permit self-interest to blur his vision. Locke is aware also that neither study of the law nor disinterestedness in applying it is common. "Yet men, being biased by their interest as well as ignorant for want of study of it, are not apt to allow of it as a law binding to them in the application of it to their particular cases."[64] The law of nature enjoins action tending to self-preservation. The urge for self-preservation is inherent in human nature. In this sense, every individual knows the law of nature. But he will not discover the dictates of this law concerning the means to self-preservation unless he studies it. There is another dimension to Locke's references to the law of nature. It denotes a certain order among things and among ideas, corresponding to an order willed by a supremely good, wise and rational God. Reason, the law of nature, is this order. It is also the capacity to comprehend this order, to accomplish it, to maintain and to defend it.[65]

In the political order, the individual is not the only bearer of inviolable rights. The civil society, though contrived, acquires, as soon as it comes into being, a nature of its own. "The first and fundamental natural law," writes Locke, "is the preservation of the society, and (*as far as will consist with the public good*) of every person in it.[66] (Italics supplied) Society, or the majority acting for it, has the right to dismiss the government, but only when the government, violating its trust, places itself in a "state of war" with the people. While it is true to its mission, neither the individual nor the society has any power against it. In the Second Essay, Locke is concerned primarily with outlawing arbitrariness. Government is precluded from treating with the people except according to laws rightfully made. But the people are likewise precluded from treating with their government arbitrarily. Within the framework of their fundamental law, the individual, the society, the government all have indefeasible rights. In Locke's theory, the individual exercises his sovereignty for the last time when he subscribes to the compact creating the civil society. His sovereignty then becomes latent and will become operative only in the unlikely and calamitous event of the civil society itself being dissolved. Except in the case of a "perfect democracy," the sovereignty of the people may likewise become latent, to be reactivated when an arbitrary government must be dismissed.

What value has the Lockean-Jeffersonian theory of local autonomy today? At the time of his visit to America, Tocqueville found that the principle of local autonomy was firmly established among the people. But the testimony of this distinguished Frenchman, even if it be, as Harold Laski has said, "perhaps the greatest work ever written on one country by the citizen of another," is now more than one and a quarter centuries old. The environment in which the locality of Tocqueville's time exercised its independence has since gone into history. Does the "amalgamation," of which he spoke, still hold? From some accounts—which are, however, essentially impressionistic—it would appear that Americans continue to cherish the legacy of Jefferson. The image of the autonomous ward republic still warms their hearts.

For example, Roscoe Martin finds that the Jeffersonian model of an agricultural republic, composed of small self–governing rural communities, is still widely respected. It is now called "grass roots." "One who rejects or ignores a grass-roots incantation does so at his peril, for the public mind does not entertain the alternative of grass-roots fallibility."[67] Admirers of grass roots argue that since in the final analysis the tasks of government are addressed to people living in the localities, these tasks should be performed by local initiative. "Stated positively, this view leads logically to the doctrine of local self-government and home rule."[68] The grass-roots concept is of course vitally associated with the individual. His view or judgment is necessarily meritorious, being invested with the prestige of grass roots. If a personal judgment happens to come from a rural setting its virtue enhances even more. "Grass roots is an expression of belief in the worth of the individual, of confidence in personal judgment. . . . In final analysis, grass roots serves as a fundamental article of the democratic faith, for *it carries the indelible impression of the sovereign individual.*"[69] (Italics supplied)

To be sure, Martin's comments relate principally to small government in rural America, where many of Jefferson's hopes continue to find fulfillment. The citizen knows the officials who perform the chores of governance. They are his friends and neighbors. If he cannot visit their offices during the day, he can transact his business with them on his doorstep, or in his home, in the evening. With the problems of government the citizen is personally acquainted. As life in the locality is simple, so is government. Politics is direct, easy-going, and informal. There is a minimum of paper work and record-keeping because "democracy is not a thing to be written down but only to be experienced."[70] Laws of a higher but "distant" government are liberally "adjusted" to the conditions and the "constitution of the place."

Another commentator, Robert C. Wood, finds the ordinary citizen still enchanted with the Jeffersonian image of the "republic-in-miniature." His attachment to it is one of the reasons that propel him towards Suburbia.[71] Arriving there, he insists on creating and retaining separate, autonomous local government. He does not wish to merge his government with that of others to form a "king-size" government for the "king-size" metropolitan community. The twentieth century American suburbanite has deliberately chosen to "retain the form of government most closely resembling Jefferson's legacy." He has made this choice in defiance of the compelling modern values of large-scale organization, efficiency, economy, rationalization. The "Great Society," laments Wood, "is excluded from his hearth and home."[72] Metropolitan reformers are now begin-

ning to discover that "it is not the simple memory of
the heritage which thwarts their efforts. It is the power
of that heritage as a very real expression of the aspirations and values of the present generation which blocks
the progress of reform."[73]

The individual is the central concern of the doctrine
of local autonomy, for it aims at preserving his inherent
and sovereign right to govern himself. The right is sovereign not only because it is "natural" but also because
its exercise leads him along the path of virtue: it imparts to him manliness and self-reliance; it teaches him
the lessons of cooperation and compromise; it sharpens
his imagination, his comprehension of the balance of
forces in society, his sense of right and wrong. Self-
government enables the individual to realize himself, to
open new vistas for the maximum development of his
capacities, to come as near perfection as human nature
will permit. Such civilization of the individual is the
summum bonum in the value system of a democratic
society. It is most likely to be attained by permitting the
individual to govern himself, which he can do most
effectively in the locality.

It is important to stress that underlying the doctrines
of the sovereignty of the individual and the independence of local government are important biases concerning
government and politics. Lurking behind all discussion of local autonomy is the notion that civil government is evil, even if a necessary evil. The stronger it is
the more wicked it is. With the Fathers of the Church,
government partook of the eternal damnation of man,
founded as it was in his incorrigibly corrupt nature.
With Jeffersonians, government is evil for the opposite
reason: it seeks to inhibit the individual who is sublime.
In order that the individual may be free and vigorous,
his government must be shackled and paralyzed. It is
true that he surrendered a part of his sovereignty to the

civil society. But, in the Jeffersonian theory, he did so for the lack of an alternative, and he has never reconciled himself to this even partial surrender. He insists that the only really active civil society be small enough so that he can in effect nullify the original grant of power to it by keeping its operations under his personal and immediate supervision and control. He denies that the civil society has any rights of its own.

The Jeffersonian theorist argues that politics, being the struggle for power, is dirty, because power is a great corrupter of humans. It does not disturb him that the power which allegedly corrupts man is that of man himself. Man expresses himself when he exercises the power that lies at his command. But if, by hypothesis, he is sublime, how can his self-expression result in corruption? Power is considered evil also because its exercise by one individual serves to limit the sovereignty of others. (The ideal state would then be one that somehow combined perpetual abundance of the means to well-being with universal impotence.) Permissible "politics" consists in conducting conference diplomacy. It brings sovereigns together so that they may make such concessions to one another as may be necessary for realizing their inter-dependent interests. The art of politics becomes the art of making "deals."

Local autonomy becomes a keystone in the structure of checks and balances designed to bring about such frustration of governmental power as will ensure the freedom of the individual. The Jeffersonian design does not seek to establish and maintain equality of power between the members of a complex balance of power system. Rather, its objective, as in most such systems, is the supremacy of one over all others, not equality. The locality is intended to emerge as the paramount center of power, and here the individual shall reign supreme!

It is not without an element of irony that the popular
American theory of government should have been
founded on the premise that government ought not to
be. It may be more than irony, however; it may be the
cardinal error of the Jeffersonian theory of local self-
government.

CHAPTER 3

Sovereign or Vassal?

That local governments are sovereign in any measure will sound blasphemous to purists among professors and practitioners of law. In most statements of the legal status of municipal corporations, one reads that sovereignty belongs to the state, not to the locality. The latter is a mere "creature," an "agent," an "instrumentality," a "department," or a "subordinate sub-division" of the state. It lives and functions by the grace and during the pleasure of its lord and master, its creator, the sovereign state. The authority of an eminent jurist, John Forrest Dillon, is invoked to support this view. Parenthetically, the reader may be informed that at one time a certain other jurist, Thomas McIntyre Cooley, held a contrary view, to wit, that localities have an inherent right to local self-government. But this view, he learns, commanded only limited judicial recognition and is now defunct. The Dillon Rule is the prevailing law of the land, confirmed several times by the Supreme Court of the United States. Among the authori-

ties quoted to clinch the matter is Judge Dillon himself.[1]

However, the difference of opinion between Judge
Dillon and Judge Cooley is not an isolated event in
American judicial history. For almost a century, scores
of cases involving rights of local governments have
come before various state supreme courts, which judges
have decided following either Dillon or Cooley. Elo-
quence and vigor of argument, explorations into history, and expositions of political theory will more generally be found in decisions belonging to the Cooley
school of thought, while the Dillon school relied mainly
upon the written constitution. The controversy occurs
as a great debate in the annals of American local government.

Judges and writers of the Cooley school assert that
from time immemorial, localities in the Anglo-Saxon
world have enjoyed the right to self-government. This
right is inherent, in that it is ancient, and ought to rank
with the other inviolable rights of the Anglo-Saxon
people. It matters not if a written constitution does not
safeguard it specifically. One may go as far back as the
Magna Charta and find that one of the guarantees that
the barons at Runnymede wrested from King John related to the "ancient liberties and free customs" of London and all other cities. The right to local self-government is "a part of the unwritten constitution, one of
the common law rights brought over from England by
our ancestors and *never surrendered.*"[2] (Italics supplied)

It is contended that a written constitution is never
wholly expressive of the fundamental law of a State. It
must be interpreted with reference to a people's settled
convictions.[3] To these the written word is subordinate.
A constitution does not create but merely acknowledges
or records the established rights of individuals and in-

stitutions. That certain rights have not been so recorded does not mean that they have been abolished.

It is indeed possible to argue that powers which the people have not expressly reserved to themselves vest in the government. But in the American tradition, which is a tradition of limited government and not that of a Hobbesian Leviathan, one ought not so to argue. Here the "better view" is that "all power is reserved to the people unless it can be found to be somewhere delegated to some department of government."[4]

Some legal scholars maintain that the American federal system consists not of two but of three levels of government: federal, state, and local. In varying degrees, sovereignty resides at all these three levels.

> The towns and cities, or other units of government, [are] also endowed with *a certain limited sovereign power* in the sense that while subject to general laws passed by the state legislature . . . they have a constitutional right, expressed or implied, to manage their own local affairs free from the interference or control of the legislature.[5]
> (Italics supplied)

It is true that the tradition of local self-government is uneven in various parts of this country. In certain areas, state control of local authorities, rather than local autonomy, has been the dominant tradition. But it is urged that regardless of a contrary tradition in American law and practice, the principle of local autonomy should be preserved against the theory of unlimited state supremacy. The maintenance of this principle is indispensable to the continuance of American liberty and democracy. For the "cradle of liberty," where citizens learn the principles and practice of democracy, is in American towns and cities, not in the states or the nation.

Such is, broadly speaking, the argument of the

Cooley school, asserting a prescriptive right to local
self-government. Since 1871 and Cooley's decision in
People v. *Hurlbut,* many other judges have quoted him
approvingly, some even praising him in the superlative.
Judge McKinstry (1875) considered him the most "distinguished expounder of constitutional law" in this
country; Judge Henderson (1903) thought that a reading of Cooley's opinions was "like sounding a new note
on the old Liberty Bell, and must inevitably thrill the
heart of every patriotic American." He answered Attorney General C. K. Bell, who had called Cooley's doctrines "politically vicious," by quoting extensively from
Cooley's works on the ground that these would "bar
the way of those who desired to overthrow the principles of local self-government."

It would be repetitious, and space-consuming, to present the opinions of all the judges who agreed with
Cooley.[6] More important, the views of Cooley himself,
the leader of the school, are submitted at length in the
following pages. Only brief reference should be made
to one or two other judges. We should first take note
of Judge Brown's dissent in *People* v. *Draper* (15 N.Y.,
1857) since it anticipated by nearly a decade and a
half important elements of Judge Cooley's classic judgment in *People* v. *Hurlbut.* Judge Brown argued that
the state constitution of 1846 had not produced a brand
new scheme of government for the people of New York.
They already had the forms and institutions of government that embodied the conventional wisdom of the
race. The new constitution intended to preserve them
and to improve them in the light of subsequent knowledge and experience, not to impair their strength or to
"deform their fair proportions." Municipalities, observed Judge Brown, were coeval with the state government. They were "institutions of the state, durable and
indestructible by any power less than that which gave
being to the organic law."[7] The state might control

them. It might increase or decrease their number or
territorial limits, annex parts of some to parts of others,
but it could not destroy or change radically their dis-
tinctive character and attributes without "confound-
ing" the entire system of constitutional government in
the state. "The state at large is, and ever has been, an
aggregate of these local bodies. They have habitually
and uninterruptedly exercised many of the powers and
functions of government."[8]

It would appear that in Judge Brown's view it is the
system of local government, self-governing in its own
proper sphere, which is inviolable; not so every township, village or hamlet. It is significant also that he
regards the "state at large" as an aggregate of the localities within its territory. They are the operating units,
the constituent members of the state as a body politic.
The ills and disorders that afflict the state cannot be
remedied by depriving individual citizens of their inherent rights, or populous and powerful communities
of their ancient franchises. In a democracy, "laws depend for their utility, their force and efficacy, upon the
enlightened moral sense of those upon whom they are
to operate; and it is as unwise as it is unwarranted to
pass acts which impair inherent rights."[9] Law must not
merely follow the forces which shape the politics of
power; it must address itself to the moral sense of the
community, and in so doing, strengthen, even elevate
that moral sense.

Judge Cooley's decision in the famous case of *People
v. Hurlbut* (24 Mich. 44, 1871) arose from the refusal
of the Water and Sewer Commissioners of the City of
Detroit to vacate their respective offices and give way
to a state appointed board of public works. The commissioners contended that the act of the state legislature, supplanting the existing city organizations for
water supply and sewage disposal, and replacing them
with a state appointed board of public works, was re-

pugnant to the state constitution. The Supreme Court
of Michigan ruled that the legislature lacked authority
to appoint city officials on a permanent basis. The
judges then proceeded, one after the other,* to express
themselves on the nature of a written constitution, and
the ancient rights of cities.

First, Chief Justice Campbell started by saying that
a constitution is not the source of a people's laws and
liberties. In the main, it is no more than a recognition
and "re-enactment" of an existing and accepted system.
Its terms have a "settled meaning" at the time of its
adoption. These meanings should not be ignored when
studying and interpreting the document subsequently.
The rights which a constitution preserves are ancient
rights. The municipalities, which the constitution of
Michigan recognized and which it required to be preserved, were not entities in the abstract. They were
real, already existing, Michigan municipalities of "common law origin and having no less than common law
franchises" with "known elements and functions."[10]
The Chief Justice went on to emphasize that in both
England and America municipalities had always been
self-governing communities within the limits of their
charters. This, he said, was no "mere political theory!"
It was the cornerstone of the American polity. "Our
constitution cannot be understood or carried out at all,
except on the theory of local self-government; and the
intention to preserve it is quite apparent."[11]

In a judgment that became widely influential, Judge
Cooley rushed through the "secondary questions" in
the case, and then settled down to stating his theory of
local self-government. He recognized that according to
the prevailing constitutional law, the state created mu-

* Judge Graves wrote only a short concurring judgment.
Judge Cristiancy's judgment was in full accord with the judgments of Chief Justice Campbell and Judge Cooley, though not
as forceful.

nicipalities and abolished them at discretion, "clothing them for the time being with a portion of its sovereignty, but recalling the whole or part thereof" when the necessity for such delegation disappeared. But such maxims, said Judge Cooley, "are very seldom true in anything more than a general sense; they never are and never can be literally accepted in practice."[12] It was true that state constitutions did not expressly require the existence everywhere of county or township organizations. Nor did they specifically prohibit the state legislatures from creating, and filling, new local offices to administer certain local affairs. From the absence of such specific prohibitions, some jurists had concluded that state legislatures could lawfully deprive the people of a locality of their right to self-government. This doctrine would startle the American people, were it to be asserted in practice!

Judge Cooley agreed with Chief Justice Campbell that the framers of the constitution had in mind certain fundamental principles. They delegated authority to the various departments of their government subject to this framework. Thus there were, in addition to specific limitations placed upon legislative power in the constitution itself, "implied restrictions" that were "equally imperative in character." If in construing the constitution, we ignored these implied restrictions, "we should fall into the grossest of absurdities." In Cooley's words,

Some things are too plain to be written. If this charter of state government which we call a constitution, were all there was of constitutional command; if the usages, the customs, the maxims that have sprung from the habits of life; modes of thought . . . the precepts which have come from the revolutions which overturned tyrannies, the sentiments of manly independence and self-control which impelled our ancestors to summon the local

community to redress local evils, instead of relying
on a king or a legislature at a distance to do so—
if a recognition of all these were to be stricken
from the body of our constitutional law, a lifeless
skeleton might remain, but the living spirit, that
which gives it force and attraction, which makes
it valuable and draws to it the affections of the
people . . . this living and breathing spirit, which
supplies the interpretation of the words of the
written charter, would be utterly lost and gone.[13]

What are those great and fundamental, if only implied, principles that underlie a written state constitution? Advancing considerable historical evidence, Judge
Cooley observes that certain parts of this country have
had a system of local self-government from the time of
the earliest settlements. In some cases, the town or the
city existed as a corporate body politic even before
there was a colonial, state, or national government.
When both the city and the state had come into being,
"they ran parallel to each other, as they were meant to
do, for all time." The tradition of local self-government
is then an integral part of the American way of life.

It is interesting that Judge Cooley relies heavily on
Tocqueville's *Democracy in America*. He quotes approvingly that writer's statement that each of the New
England townships "originally formed an independent
nation." Again, with approval clearly implicit, he
quotes Tocqueville's following observation: "It is important that they [townships] have not been invested
with privileges, *but that they seem on the contrary, to
have surrendered* a portion of their independence to the
state."[14] (Italics supplied) Cooley construes this to
mean that the states received delegated powers from
independent towns. He admits that this is not the generally accepted theory, which holds that the state pre-
ceded the locality and created it at its discretion. But

the prevailing theory, he adds, is historically inaccurate. While cautious in endorsing Tocqueville's observation, Judge Cooley's inclination to laud him is apparent.

Another great underlying principle of American state constitutions is that the locality is the "cradle" and also the guardian of American liberty and democracy. Judge Cooley recalls that the localities in the eastern and middle states contributed significantly towards defeating the attempts of the last two Stuart kings to overthrow American liberties. When colonial charters were being withdrawn or suspended, representatives of the people in Massachusetts insisted that "to surrender local government was contrary to the sixth commandment, for, said they, 'men may not destroy their political any more than their natural lives.' "[15] Again, as Jefferson acknowledged in a letter to Governor Tyler in 1810, Americans owed to "these little republics" the vigor of their Revolution. Such being the "historical facts" regarding local government in the United States, municipalities exercise their franchises under the protection of fundamental principles which no power in the state can override or disregard. Concluded Judge Cooley: "The state may mould local institutions according to its views of policy or expediency: *but local government is a matter of absolute right,* and the state cannot take it away."[16] (Italics supplied)

In his two major works, *Constitutional Limitations* and *The General Principles of Constitutional Law,* Cooley reiterated the main thesis of *People* v. *Hurlbut.* Unlike societies where governmental powers were concentrated at the center, "complete decentralization" characterized the American system of government. Here the controlling principle was that local authorities should manage local affairs and the central government should concern itself with "general affairs" only. Accordingly, the states yielded to the national government

only such powers over domestic affairs as were essential
to the maintenance of their union. The same principle
impelled them to divide their territory into units of local
government and confer upon them powers of local legislation. "The system is one which almost seems a part
of the very nature of the race to which we belong."[17]
The various state constitutions assumed the continued
existence of local government. The state could, without
doubt, control local governments, but there were limits
to its power in this respect as in others.

> Some of these [limits] are expressly defined; others
> spring from the usages, customs, and maxims of
> our people; they are a part of its history, a part
> of the system of local self–government, in view of
> the continuance and perpetuity of which all our
> constitutions are framed, and of the right to which
> the people can never be deprived except through
> express renunciation on their part.[18]

In *People* v. *Hurlbut* Judge Cooley had conceded
that the state could "mould local institutions according
to its views of policy or expediency." He reasserts this
part of his argument in the works now under reference.
The form of local government and the extent of its
powers cannot be fixed once for all. These must vary
according to circumstances: the governmental structure
and powers necessary for a city of one million people
cannot be the same as those of a country hamlet. In its
wisdom and prudence, the state will confer upon local
governments such powers as may appear to be expedient. At any time it may even abolish a certain local
government unit and establish another in its stead. In
sum, "while the local community is entitled to local
government, it cannot claim, as against the state, any
particular charter or form of local government."[19]

From the tenor and the spirit that pervade Cooley's

works it would follow that the state's discretionary power over local government should be exercised with caution and with due regard to the usages, maxims and modes of thought of the people. He is not opposed to change, but he is very much concerned with the rate of change. Change should not be abrupt or radically large. As the maxims and the modes of thought of the people change so the state might change the local government scene within its territory. But at any given time, it may do no more than tinker with local institutions. It is interesting that despite his frequent insistence that the federal constitution ought not to change in response to new circumstances or crises, unless amended, he was aware that the power of the federal government had expanded much beyond the limits envisaged in 1787 and that it would continue to expand. Institutions, he wrote, did not stand still. Moreover, "power, when it has attained a certain degree of energy and independence, goes on generally to further progress."[20] The regulatory power of the United States over inter-state commerce had become applicable to railroads, telegraph and the telephone. The sheer immensity of the interests coming under federal control would inevitably conduce to even further enlargements of federal power.

Cooley's theory of local self-government is of a piece with his general political theory and his overall view of the American system of government. That sovereignty resides in the people is a fundamental principle of government in this country, he observes. "According to American ideas it is the only true theory, which because it is true ought to be accepted as a foundation fact everywhere. . . ."[21] Although sovereignty is often defined as a "supreme, absolute, and uncontrollable power" in an independent State, it is actually subject to limitations. Neither the government nor the people can do any and all things. Express constitutional limitations and implied restrictions circumscribe the sovereignty of the people.

The state is a voluntary association of individuals made for their convenience and for preserving their rights. The "police power" of the state is therefore not a progressive or active power. It is rather a protective and conservative power, "calculated to prevent a conflict of rights and to insure to each [individual] the uninterrupted enjoyment of his own, so far as is reasonably consistent with a like enjoyment of rights by others."[22] It is not appropriate for a free government to interfere with the ordinary course of economic activity in society. It ought not to fix prices or undertake economic enterprises. These should be left to private initiative and management. Judge Cooley deplored "class legislation" and advised labor to recognize and accept the "laws of political economy."

A laissez-faire conservative, Cooley became a major contributor to the development of laissez-faire constitutionalism in this country. In a notable analysis of "How Laissez Faire Came to the Supreme Court," Mr. Benjamin Twiss observes that Cooley's book, *A Treatise on the Constitutional Limitations Which Rest Upon the Legislative Power of the States of the American Union,* was published in 1868 "almost as a direct counter to the appearance a year earlier of Karl Marx's *Das Kapital.*"[23] According to Professor Corwin, and many others, it was a vastly influential book, quickly becoming the most frequently quoted authority on American constitutional law.[24] Cooley indicated at considerable length the areas of state power and discretion, but he was concerned mainly with pointing out the limitations that rested upon that power. In the preface to his book, he professed to have written in full sympathy with all those restraints which the caution of the fathers had imposed upon the exercise of the powers of government, and with faith in the checks and balances of our republican system.

Judge Cooley entertained the traditional American distrust of power and partook of the conservative fear of the political power of the masses and "mobs." He saw an inherent antagonism between governmental power, having an inevitable tendency towards self-aggrandizement, and the rights of the individual. He believed in the "laws of political economy," that is, in laissez faire. The attempted subversion of these "laws" by many state legislatures, that were enacting "class legislation" and were competing with the individual entrepreneur by investing borrowed money in various publicly owned and operated enterprises (railroads, canals, steamship lines, manufactures), confirmed his belief in the imperative necessity of limiting governmental power.* The right to local government was thus important not only because it was an ancient right but also because it constituted a balance to the power of the state just as the rights of the states constituted a balance to the power of the federal government.

More than a decade before the celebrated Dillon Rule[25] was enunciated in Iowa, Chief Justice Denio and Justice Shankland of the New York Supreme Court announced the doctrine of state legislative "omnipo-

---

* In Cooley's day, men of substance in this country were greatly apprehensive at the current expressions of social unrest —labor strikes, farmers' agitations, increasing governmental intervention in matters economic, and the general clamor for reform. The sovereign people, under Jacksonian influence, were seen invading the sacred right to property and liberty of contract and misusing the power to tax. Socialism seemed to be close at hand. Unable to combat these "nefarious" trends, the conservatives appealed to the courts, which had been the traditional defenders of vested rights. Armed with Cooley's *Constitutional Limitations,* lawyers and judges responded to the call and wrote the doctrine of laissez faire into American constitutional law.

tence" in relation to local governments in *The People ex. rel. Fernando Wood* v. *Simeon Draper* (15 N.Y. 532, 1857). At issue was the constitutional validity of a law of April 15, 1857, whereby the state legislature had abolished the local police organizations of New York City and Brooklyn, replacing them with a Metropolitan Police District, which embraced the whole of New York City and parts of the counties of Kings, Richmond, and Worcester. This new district was headed by a commission whose members were appointed by the Governor and Senate. Some citizens of New York City looked upon these proceedings as an unprecedented and unwarranted act of interference in their domestic affairs. They marched in procession, led by their Mayor, Fernando Wood, and resisted unsuccessfully the enforcement of the law. Blood was shed. The city then appealed to the courts, but in this quarter it found little solace. The Supreme Court ruled that the legislative act in question was perfectly valid, among other reasons, because "the people, in framing the constitution, committed to the legislature the whole law making power of the state, which they did not expressly or impliedly withhold."²⁶ Judge Shankland went even further in confining the "powers reserved to the people."

The legislative power is *omnipotent* within its proper sphere. The legislature in this respect, is the *direct representative* of the people, and the delegate and depository of their power. Hence, the limitations of the *constitution are not so much limitations of the legislature as of the power of the people themselves,* self-imposed by the constitutional compact. When the court declares a law unconstitutional, it in effect declares that the *sovereign* power of the people has so far been abdicated by themselves. (Italics supplied)²⁷

Attorneys for the City pleaded that the state law at issue offended section 2 of article 10 of the state constitution, authorizing local governments to elect or appoint their own officers. The Court overruled them, saying that the constitution safeguarded the said right with reference only to offices which existed when the constitution was adopted. It did not preclude the legislature from creating new local offices and filling them.

By a law of March 26, 1860, the legislature of Iowa authorized a railroad company to build a line which would pass through the city of Clinton. It permitted the company to take over, without paying compensation, as much of the city streets as it might need for completing the project. Clinton sought judicial intervention, and the matter finally reached the state Supreme Court. The Court ruled against the city, mainly on the ground that it did not possess a property right in its streets.

M. H. Tyrrell, one of the counsel for the city, argued that the state law amounted to changing the charter of Clinton without its consent. This the legislature had no right to do, for "the King, or State, cannot force a new charter upon a municipality, nor abridge its powers." In support of his position, he cited several English cases, especially *Rex* v. *Vice-Chancellor, etc. of Cambridge* (3 Burr 1656-1661), where Chief Justice Lord Mansfield had observed that a corporation already in being did not have to accept a new charter *in toto*. "They may act partly under it, and partly under their old charter or *prescription*."[28] In other words, the state could not abolish the rights which a city held under "prescriptive usage" by amending its charter. "If the king may not abridge one power," asked Mr. Tyrrell, "how can he abolish all the privileges of a municipality?" The counsel was advancing the familiar argument that the traditional rights of individuals and institutions remained inviolable even if the written constitution did not specifically protect them. The "prescriptive constitution" sustained them.

Chief Justice Dillon replied that the English authorities cited were inapplicable to the powers of a legislature in this country. The latter might incorporate a place without its consent and likewise might qualify, increase, decrease, or even abolish its municipal powers. Thus dismissing the matter of rights under "prescriptive usage," he expounded the view that became the famous Dillon Rule:

> The true view is this: Municipal corporations owe their origin to, and derive their powers and rights *wholly* from, the legislature. It breathes into them the breath of life, without which they cannot exist. *As it creates, so it may destroy.* If it may destroy, it may abridge and control. Unless there is some constitutional limitation on the right, the legislature might by a single act, if we can suppose it capable of *so great a folly and so great a wrong,* sweep from its existence all of the municipal corporations in the State, and the corporations could not prevent it. . . . They are, so to phrase it, the mere tenants at will of the legislature.[29] (Italics supplied)

In deciding the case, the Chief Justice relied upon relevant statutes. He did not probe into the general history of the rights of municipal corporations in the Anglo–Saxon world. Indeed, he brushed aside Tyrrell's reference to such history as being irrelevant and out of order. Nor did he appeal to political theory. Nevertheless, his judgment contained an important political theory: that embodied in his "true view" of the status of municipalities.[30]

The opinion of Chief Justice Dillon is significant in more ways than one. Its influence has been pervasive. Writers on local government, lawyers, judges have

quoted it times without number. Its emphases, its metaphor, and its phrases appear in the opinions of other
courts.* But also noteworthy is the observation that the
legislature may sweep the municipalities out of existence, "if we can suppose it capable of so great a folly
and so great a wrong." Folly? Perhaps yes, from the
standpoint of administrative convenience. But why a
"great wrong?" It would appear that in employing these
words Judge Dillon was making a moral alongside a
legal judgment. Could it be that in his view the locality
had a moral right to existence even if it had no such
right in the contemplation of law, construed correctly,
that is strictly? We find a measure of support for this

* For illustration, a few judgments may be noted: Municipal
corporations "are called into being at the pleasure of the state
and the same voice which speaks them into existence can speak
them out." *Ewing* v. *Hoblitzelle,* 85 Mo. 77 (1884).

"The legislature . . . may also confer on such corporations
such public powers and authority as it may deem wise and best.
Moreover, it may not only create such public corporations, but
it may also change, divide, abolish them at pleasure." *Harris* v.
Wm. R. Compton Bond and Mortgage Co., 244 Mo. 688–89
(1912).

Municipalities are "political sub-divisions" of the state, de-
riving all their powers from the state, "mere creatures of the
state," exercising delegated functions which the legislature may
"revoke at will." *Booten* v. *Pinson,* 77 W. Va. 412 (1915).

The powers of cities "may be qualified, enlarged or withdrawn
at the pleasure of the legislature." *Reno* v. *Stoddard,* 40 Nev.
537 (1917).

"Municipal corporations are purely the creatures of the legislative will . . . and may be created or annuled at the pleasure
of the body creating them and their property turned over to
some other municipal corporation and their powers and duties
conferred upon such body." *Rylands* v. *Clark,* 278 Ill. 44–45
(1917).

"Political powers conferred by the legislature upon a municipality cannot become a vested right as against its creator. . . .
Municipal grants of franchises are always subject to the control
of the legislative power for the purpose of amendment, modifi-
cation or entire revocation." *Smiddy* v. *Memphis,* 140 Tenn. 97
(1918). See also citations in the following pages.

suggestion from a statement in his *Commentaries on the Law of Municipal Corporations.* There, after noting that the state exercises a large authority in determining the framework and powers of local governments, he goes on to say: "but while it [the state] may shape the local institutions, it cannot abolish them, and, without substituting others, take all authority to itself."[31] Why not, if it breathes into them the breath of life, if "as it creates, so it may destroy?" Perhaps even Judge Dillon did not feel entirely comfortable with the doctrine of absolute state sovereignty over local governments.

The Supreme Court of the United States also follows the Dillon Rule. In *Trenton* v. *New Jersey* (262 U.S. 182), which concerned the right of Trenton to divert water from the Delaware River for its own use beyond a per capita maximum prescribed by the state, Justice Butler, writing for the Court, declared: "In the absence of state constitutional provisions safeguarding it to them, municipalities have no inherent right of self-government which is beyond the legislative control of the state."[32] A municipality, he continued, was merely a "department" of the state. The latter could grant or withhold, increase or decrease its powers and privileges as it saw fit. However great or small a certain municipality's sphere of action, it remained "the creature of the state," holding and exercising its powers subject to the sovereign will. The Court quoted from one of its earlier opinions, which is remarkable for its trenchant quality:

> The number, nature and duration of the powers conferred upon these corporations and the territory over which they shall be exercised rests in the *absolute discretion* of the state. . . . The state, therefore, at its pleasure, may modify or withdraw all such powers . . . expand or contract the territorial area, unite the whole or a part of it with another municipality, repeal the charter and de-

stroy the corporation. All this may be done . . .
*with or without the consent of the citizens, or even
against their protest.* . . . The power is in the state
and those who legislate for the state are alone
responsible for any unjust or oppressive exercise
of it.[33] (Italics supplied)

How did the proposition become established that
state governments are absolutely sovereign over the
localities? The explanation may be found in the American political and legal tradition, the prevailing socioeconomic conditions, and the public sentiment. Proceed-
ing from the theory of popular sovereignty, inherited
from the revolutionary period and held in high popular esteem ever since, most state supreme courts
interpreted the powers of state legislatures liberally
even when these tended to encroach upon vested rights.
At the United States Supreme Court, Marshall and
Story interpreted the federal constitution liberally in
determining the powers of the federal government. The
rule of liberal construction thus prevailed in both the state
and federal courts. During the greater part of the
nineteenth century, the opposite rule, that of strict
construction, had few adherents. It is true that Marshall
and Story construed state powers strictly when these
seemed to them to transgress vested rights of individuals
and corporations or the area of federal power. But the
disposition of the Supreme Court changed when Roger
Brooke Taney became the Chief Justice. This reversal
at the Court, which now consisted largely of Southern
Democrats, is only partly attributable to its view of the
nature of the Union. Partly it must be attributed to its
activist and (in the present day jargon) "liberal" theory
of the role of government in society. The government
that governed the least was not necessarily the best.
Taney and some of his colleagues at the Court, like a
great many judges in state courts, regarded government
as an instrument of the sovereign people which the lat-

ter had every right to employ for promoting their well-being. Relating the spirit of the times, Andrew C. McLaughlin writes:

> There was enthusiasm for social betterment. Reform was in the air. Governments were no longer considered merely necessary burdens to be endured; they were expected to obey the popular will. . . . The states, Taney believed with all his heart, had not only rights but duties. It was the business of the states and their governments . . . to promote the happiness of their people; for such purposes they existed. In carrying out these duties, they should not be hindered by vague implications and presumptions gathered from the Constitution by clever interpretation. . . . That the tendency arose from an attitude of mind which was not the possession of a particular judge of a particular court is evidenced by the fact that *the state courts were moving in the same direction*.[34] (Italics supplied)

The states entered the economic domain both as entrepreneurs and regulators. The laws they passed seemed sometimes to invade personal rights to property and liberty. But the courts tended generally to treat state laws as expressions of the will of the sovereign people. They were reluctant to curb the sovereign by invoking limitations that might be implicit in the "spirit of free institutions," the doctrines of social compact and natural rights. The judges in *Mobile* v. *Yuille* voiced the prevailing judicial view when they held that they could not overrule the acts of the state legislature, made for the good of the people, merely on the ground that "they are unwise, or not in accordance with just and enlightened views of political economy, as understood at the present day."[35] In the Charles River Bridge case, Taney declared that he would not resort to "vague" presumptions to prevent the state from meeting the constantly arising new socio-economic needs of its people.

> . . . the object and end of all government is to promote the happiness and prosperity of the community by which it was established. . . . The continued existence of a government would be of no great value, if by implications and presumptions, it was disarmed of the powers necessary to accomplish the ends of its creation, and the functions it was designed to perform, transferred to the hands of privileged corporations.[36]

Such was the influence of popular sovereignty in judicial councils that Justice Story feared the day might never come again when an American court would declare a state or federal law unconstitutional. "A change has come over the public mind from which I augur little good," he lamented.

However, towards the end of the nineteenth century, the tide turned. The theory of implicit constitutional limitations upon governmental power began to find favor with the courts and dominated them for several decades. Under the spell of laissez faire, advocates of the rights of the individual and corporations held the sovereign people at bay. But municipal corporations did not benefit from the new climate of opinion. Although the movement for municipal home rule began and gained strength in the political sphere, judges continued to uphold complete state sovereignty over local governments.*

* It ought to be clear that the theory of popular sovereignty that the judges saluted is not the same as the Jeffersonian theory of the sovereignty of the people. In that theory the people's sovereignty is eventually translated into the individual's sovereignty. The judges under reference would appear rather to have been influenced by the latter-day American theorists of sovereignty to whom reference was made earlier and by European thinkers.

A most interesting case in point is that of *State* v. *Thompson* (149 Wis. 488, 1912). In 1911 the legislature of Wisconsin passed a "Home Rule" act, authorizing every city to alter or amend its charter. In sweeping language, section I of the act declared every city "to have all powers in relation to the form of its government, and to the conduct of its municipal affairs not in contravention of . . . the constitution or laws, operative generally throughout the state." Pursuant to this act, the City Council of Milwaukee sought an amendment to the city charter that would permit it to make and sell ice. The Council ordered the City Clerk, a Mr. Thompson, to submit the proposed amendment to the people of Milwaukee. This Thompson refused to do on the ground that the enabling law was unconstitutional. The City Council sought and obtained a writ of mandamus, instructing Thompson to submit the matter to the people. He appealed to the state Supreme Court, which vacated the lower court's order.

After chastising the advocates and antagonists of home rule, who were "more enthusiastic than thoughtful," for publishing "much crude and ill-digested information," Judge Timlin of Wisconsin proceeded to formulate a theory of sovereignty. It was elementary, he observed, that there could be only one sovereign power in the government of a state. "As well might we speak of two centers in a circle as of two sovereign powers in a state."[37] True that in this country, sovereignty had been divided between the Union and the states, but even in such situations, a clash between the two sovereignties was inevitable unless there be an "overlord empowered to determine what matters belong under the jurisdiction of each sovereign." The government possessing this overlordship was "the real sovereign."[38]

Judge Timlin noted that laws and institutions were sustained by their determining causes. When the underlying cause disappeared, the institution or the rule, which had appeared in response to it, would crumble. Laws relating to the autonomous government of American cities could not be valid unless they answered the fundamental conditions of government. And in order to be effective, they must not only be valid but also "appropriate to sociological and political conditions existing here, not to those existing elsewhere, and they must respond to our changing conditions."[39] The Dillon Rule was a correct statement of the law, he emphasized, and it must finally prevail:

> It can in no way be avoided so long as our present system of federal and state governments obtains and so long as *these underlying forces operate which always tend to lodge ultimate sovereign power with him best able to exercise it and whose position makes him the final arbiter of his own claim to such power*. This is the state, not the city. There can be no absolute autonomy in American cities no matter how limited the subject.[40] (Italics supplied)

Life is a struggle, Judge Timlin emphasized. Spoils then belong to the victor. Sovereignty resides with those who can exercise it.

Whatever one may think of the legal virtue of Judge Timlin's observations, and of their amoral emphases, one must admire him for making an interesting innovation away from the beaten track of the argument along the Dillon Rule. Coming from a judge, the innovation is all the more refreshing. Judge Timlin's view has many adherents among contemporary writers on local government; it will be considered later in these pages.

CHAPTER 4

Government by the People

In the post-Civil War period, many state legislatures, weakened materially by the successive waves of constitutional limitations of their authority, succumbed to the pressures of political bosses and corporate magnates. They passed much "ripper" legislation for the benefit of a variety of franchise hunters, building contractors, and patronage-hungry politicians. A reaction was not long in coming. Two popular movements arose to "restore" government to the people: the movement for direct legislation and that for municipal home rule. The quarter century from 1890 to the beginning of World War I would appear to be especially noteworthy for an intensive consideration of these matters. Professors, statesmen, reformers, politicians discussed their pros and cons. Let us first consider the debate over direct legislation.

Direct legislation. In 1898 the constitution of South Dakota authorized voters to make ordinary local and state laws and to pronounce upon laws made by legis-

latures through the processes of the initiative and referendum.* Soon a number of states followed suit: Utah
(1900), Oregon (1902), Nevada (1904), Montana
(1906), Oklahoma (1907), Maine (1908), Missouri
(1909), Arkansas and Colorado (1910), and Arizona
and California (1911).[1] Direct legislation gained acceptance in both local and state governments. In 1912 William B. Munro wrote that of the two hundred or so
cities that had adopted the commission form of government all except those in Texas had provided also the
initiative and referendum.[2] The proponents of direct
legislation came mostly from the ranks of the "progressives." Some of them wanted to restore to the people
their right to self-government. Others sought to reestablish "representative government" by making legislatures more responsive to the people. They wanted to
wipe out the corrupting influence of city bosses and
privilege-seeking businessmen from the existing legislatures. The opponents of direct legislation feared that
the evils which the reformers wished to cure would be
aggravated if direct legislation became a part of the
American system.

George W. Guthrie, once mayor of Pittsburgh, and
Robert Treat Paine[3] maintained that the municipal referendum would make the people directly sovereign—
a perfectly appropriate development, for in a democracy sovereignty belonged to the people alone and could

* In America, the initiative and referendum are as old as the
country itself. Even when the legislatures took over the main
responsibility for making ordinary statute law, the voters,
through the referendum, still pronounced upon constitutional
proposals. They made statute law by writing into the state constitutions detailed provisions for all kinds of contingencies. During the eighteenth century several state constitutions, e. g.
Massachusetts, Pennsylvania and New Hampshire, reserved to
the people the right to instruct their representatives in the state
legislature. William B. Munro, ed., *The Initiative, Referendum
and Recall* (New York: D. Appleton, 1912), p. 6.

not be delegated to "any body or department." Professor Lewis Jerome Johnson wrote that the people must assert their "natural right" to revise the work of their legislators, especially where the latter had failed to do the public will. It was not intended to abolish legislatures; they would remain. They would not have the last word, but then "final enacting power is far from essential to the dignity of a legislative body."[4] Its members were after all merely agents of the people.

The people, Johnson thought, would not be called upon to make laws often, but the mere existence of their power to veto legislative measures would produce many wholesome results. Log-rolling would disappear, and the pernicious influence of franchise-hunters and political bosses would be eradicated. The representative system would "enter upon a period of honor and usefulness." High-minded and able individuals would then seek legislative office. They would be re-elected any number of times. The individual would come in touch with the great affairs of State and thus gain in maturity and wisdom. By voting for "measures apart from men, and for men apart from measures," he would begin to "assume the stature of a man, to become a sovereign in fact as well as in fancy."[5]

Johnson did not share the apprehension that direct legislation would result in inexpedient legislation or lead to mob rule. The opposite indeed might be expected. Providing the people with adequate means of expressing and implementing their will was in the long run the only "preventive of violent upheavals." The method of direct legislation was part of the American tradition. Changes of scene and circumstance could not destroy its validity or merit. Its use need not be limited to small communities. "A sound fundamental principle holds regardless of the scale of the enterprise. That a self-governing people must have effective control over the laws under which they live would seem to be a principle of this kind."[6]

Jonathan Bourne, Jr., United States Senator from Oregon, justified direct legislation in terms of "rights of men" and the sovereignty of the individual, adding, however, a touch of utilitarian logic to the argument. Men, he said, acted on the basis of "impulse" or "deduction." The voter, given adequate time to consider matters, as he was in initiative proceedings, would reason his way to a decision. In this he might be influenced by selfish considerations, for men were selfish too. But when men acted collectively their selfish interests canceled one another out so that the net result, through the working of an invisible hand, as it were, was promotive of the general interest and not of partial or special interests. The selfish individual, contained by other selfish individuals, had to settle for his "proportional" share in the improved general welfare. The greatest good of the greatest number was thus served.[7]

Bourne maintained that a system of direct legislation would be more honest and competent than a system of "delegated government."[8] In the former the public servant owed allegiance and responsibility to the community as a whole whereas in the latter he owed these to specific individuals and groups: bosses, caucuses, conventions, campaign contributors. The people were more honest than their representatives in city councils. If occasionally they sold their votes, they did so in a mood of despair and helplessness in the face of entrenched civic evils. Deliberating in the quiet of their homes, the voters would make better and more progressive laws than did the legislatures. Addressing the American Academy of Political and Social Science, the Senator observed that direct legislation would serve the following purposes: restore the sovereignty of the people; educate and develop the people; secure legislation for the general welfare; prevent legislation against the gen-

eral welfare; eliminate the legislative blackmailer; make
our legislative bodies truly representative.[9]

Professor John R. Commons saw two broad tasks
confronting local government. First was the problem of
giving the people their due share in the benefits of technological progress, then there was the problem of making city government more honest and efficient. These
two tasks, the political and the administrative, were
distinct and separate and must be performed by separate agents so that they might be performed well. The
initiative and referendum provided the machinery for
achieving the desired separation. "They provide a means
outside the administration for the discussion and settlement of questions of policy, questions of class interest,
questions of distribution of wealth and privilege, questions of control over morals, beliefs and enjoyments.
. . . They separate the political from the business
problem."[10]

A city council could not settle these questions. It
lacked the necessary prestige. It had been overshadowed
by the mayor, and it had fallen into the hands of special
interests. They would be better settled in a popular
referendum where, because of their large number and
diversity, none of the contending special interests could
prevail. Relieved of the authority to make political decisions and of the power to dispense privilege, city administrators would be liberated from political bosses
and organized special interests. The people themselves,
having obtained control of the distribution of wealth
and privilege, would have no further use for political
bosses. Commons did not think that the people would
have to declare their will frequently.

The questions of policy, though all important and
basic, are not continuously up for solution. Administration is much the larger part of municipal government in point of time occupied, though not in

point of popular passions excited. The political
questions arise only on somewhat rare occasions,
and a settlement once reached . . . guides the administration for years.[11]

Theodore Roosevelt and Woodrow Wilson viewed
the initiative and referendum largely as a protest movement, an expression of anger at the failure of state
legislatures to represent the people and serve their interests. If genuine representative government were available in the states and the localities, no one would want
the initiative and referendum. The emergence of these
institutions, they hoped, would rectify the existing
defects of legislative bodies. Roosevelt defined the virtues of a representative closely following the Burkean
model. He warned that the initiative and referendum
should not be used "wantonly or in a spirit of levity."
The people were not capable of handling any large
number of legislative proposals. Moreover, they were
fickle![12]

Wilson shared Roosevelt's view that the initiative
and referendum should be used sparingly. He cautioned
that the American people had already overextended
themselves in trying to check and control government.
They had made practically every office in government
elective. They were clearly unable to perform the enormous job of filling all these offices at frequent intervals.
The political machine and the boss had arisen to manage the business of politics which the people had created but failed to manage. Government by town meeting was a thing of the past, said Wilson, feasible only
in small homogeneous communities. Americans, he
thought, did not want to cut themselves loose from
their past tradition. They were resorting to direct legislation to force upon their representatives the consciousness that their duty was to represent and serve
the people and not the private interests "which creep

into their counsels by way of machine orders and committee conferences."[13]

Direct legislation also had many opponents. Notable
among them were: A. Lawrence Lowell, Gamaliel
Bradford, Ellis P. Oberholtzer, Albert B. Hart, Henry
Jones Ford, William B. Munro, John B. Sanborn,
George H. Haynes, Charles M. Hollingsworth, and
Samuel W. McCall. The views of McCall, Hollingsworth and Munro are presented below, since together
they provide a fairly complete statement of the case
against direct legislation.

Congressman McCall did not rate highly the "common man's" integrity or ability, or even his interest in
governmental affairs. The voter was no more honest
than his representative in a legislature. Organized interests could buy signatures on initiative petitions by the
"car load." Nor would the voter abandon his private
pursuits to study questions of public policy. The vast
majority of the people would most likely pronounce
upon a proposed law without even reading it. Indeed,
many of the bad laws coming out of the state legislatures had resulted from the "overzeal of representatives
to respond to the transient and noisy . . . manifestations
of popular opinion."[14] The essentials of the legislative
process—deliberation, "common counsel," debate, compromise—would be lost in direct legislation. The people could best perform only the function of choosing
their representatives. Having chosen them, they should
let the representatives serve the common interest according to the dictates of their conscience and best
judgment. Representatives should be "statesmen," not
mere politicians. Quoting from Burke's renowned
Bristol speech,* the Congressman observed that a representative should not look only to the "flash of the
day" or bow to every "prevailing fancy." He should do

* See Chapter 8.

his duty as he sees it from the "elevated point of view provided by his office."

McCall warned that direct legislation would further weaken state legislatures by depriving them of the final power of making laws. Legislators would dodge their duty to oppose bad but specious legislation on the spurious ground that they wanted guidance from the "supreme court" of public opinion. Political cowardice and corruption would increase. McCall concluded that direct legislation was a primitive, not progressive, form of government. Representative government, being truly modern and progressive, was the only way, as the Founding Fathers had taught, of governing a large and populous territory. They knew that excessive dilution and dispersion of governmental power would lead to anarchy and eventually to despotism.

Charles M. Hollingsworth agreed with McCall that the primitive system of direct legislation would finally usher in the absolute rule of the "man on horseback." It was undemocratic in its "basis and objects" and unconstitutional in its spirit. Its champions, the "so-called progressives," were not interested in the whole people but only in the "plain people," the "common people," the "masses"—that is, in people who had little or no wealth. They opposed the large economic interests and wanted to deprive them of any determining voice in government.[15] Conceding that these economic interests had perverted representative government, the progressive remedy was equally perverse. It induced the "plain people" to vote large plenary, and essentially arbitrary, powers into the hands of "single individuals." The beneficiaries of the people's favor were the demagogues who led and managed the direct legislation movement. Such individuals—for instance, Mr. U'Ren of Oregon who, according to the *Portland Oregonian,* carried under his hat one of Oregon's two legislatures—inevitably rose to power because the people themselves

were quite incapable of making laws. The direct legislation system thus conferred law-making power upon
self-appointed, non-official, extra-constitutional law
makers who exercised power without being responsible
to anyone. They were bosses, albeit of a new type.
Direct legislation, Hollingsworth warned, would increase corruption among the people, arbitrariness and
inefficiency in government. It would exclude capable
and self-respecting men from public office. Statesmen
would depart from the political scene, leaving it to
politicians![16]

William B. Munro also viewed the direct legislation
movement as a gesture of protest from which little good
and much harm might result. Having lost faith in the
ability and integrity of elected legislators, the people
were now bent upon taking away from the "wicked and
slothful servant" what little power he had. They did
not realize that the legislature's incompetence and its
subservience to powerful "sinister" interests resulted
from its lack of centralized and energetic leadership.
Nor did they understand that a body "which can do no
harm can, by the same token, do little good." Volumi-
nous constitutions, providing for most fundamental
questions of policy and even many matters of administrative detail, had already relegated state legislatures
to the task of looking after "odds and ends." Numerous
constitutional and charter amendments had destroyed
the finality of legislative power in many respects; "direct
legislation would destroy it in all." The logical thing
for the people to do was to elect men of sufficient ability
and integrity to legislative office. But the people were
not inclined to be logical in the protests they made.
They would change the system but not their own ways.
"The demos postulates its own infallibility."[17]

Munro maintained that the people were best able to
say "yes" or "no" to questions put to them. They could
not reason together or profit from the give and take

of debate. Confronted with a large number of questions, they would take the advice of a leader or a boss. Moreover, decisions made through direct legislation would reflect the views and wishes of financially strong and organized minorities. The interest of the "unaffiliated citizen" would suffer.[18] Elected officials were not merely agents of the voter. Their functions went beyond reflecting their constituents' views, which were often "perfunctory and erratic," subject to "fleeting passion," and contrary to the "ultimate interests of the community."[19]

A few other opponents of direct legislation may be noticed in passing. Gamaliel Bradford dismissed the initiative as the "wildest work of a disordered imagination."[20] President Lowell and Henry Jones Ford feared that direct legislation would obstruct progressive legislation. Laws passed in the interest of the working class might be held up or even defeated by the employers' call for a referendum.[21] Oberholtzer saw the initiative and referendum as agencies of "socialist agitators" for enacting "class legislation." With these the "reformer" expected to "beat the heads of the slower-going parts of the population—the college trained, the reflecting, the established property-holding parts of the nation."[22] All this in the name of the "people," who had already demonstrated their inability even to elect able and honest men to legislatures. "It is always the people— the people who have brought on three of the wars in which the nation can feel the least pride, who have repeatedly attacked proper money systems, who in ignorance and on impulse have wrecked and ruined . . . a series of mistakes as long as history itself."[23] The Founding Fathers, said Oberholtzer, had deliberately rejected direct democracy. They had expected that the "wisest and best" from among the people would be chosen to lead and govern. They never thought that the public servant would be stripped of his authority and made a "puppet" of popular "whim." The progres-

sive would not only give the alien, the Negro, the poor
and the ignorant the right to vote for elective office
but also the right to make, interpret and enforce the
law. This might all be democratic; unfortunately, it was
also un-American and un-English![24]

Needless to say, Oberholtzer's observation that direct
legislation is un-American and un-English is only partly
correct. Jefferson's preference for direct democracy is
well-known. In his *Common Sense,* Tom Paine wrote
that when a community was ready for self-government,
"some convenient tree will afford them a state house
under the branches of which the whole colony may assemble to deliberate on public matters." Representatives, when they must be had, should have the same
concerns as their electors and should act in the same
manner "as the whole body would act were they present." But it is probably correct that in this matter, as
in many others, Jefferson and Paine get their inspiration from revolutionary France, not from conservative
England. It will be recalled that Rousseau's ideal democracy also functioned under a tree (an oak, to be specific). The "general will" must speak for itself. Its
sovereignty could not be represented any more than it
could be alienated. In *The Social Contract* (Book III),
he declared:

> The deputies of the people, therefore, are not and
> cannot be their representatives; they can only be
> their commissioners, and as such are not qualified
> to conclude anything definitely. No act of theirs
> can be a law, unless it has been ratified by the
> people in person; and without that ratification
> nothing is a law. The people of England deceive
> themselves when they fancy they are free; they are
> so, in fact, only during the election of members of
> parliament: for, as soon as a new one is elected,
> they are again in chains, and are nothing.

Municipal Home Rule. In 1875 Missouri amended its constitution, authorizing St. Louis to frame a charter for its own government. By 1925 fifteen states had followed Missouri's example. In subsequent years still other states granted some of their cities constitutional home rule. This, however, did not mean that home rule cities could do what they liked. By and large, city government remained a government of enumerated powers. Even when the state legislature granted cities broad powers, the courts narrowed them down.

The National Municipal League has been a consistent advocate of municipal home rule from its inception in 1894. One of its prominent members, Horace E. Deming, maintained that the people must have a "direct and controlling" influence upon their government which, in turn, must express and do their will. City governments did not command the respect of their citizens, and failed to arouse feelings of local pride and patriotism among them, because they lacked the authority to serve their needs and interests. Cities would not be governed well unless they were self-governing, until the "outside authority," the state legislature, stopped meddling in their affairs. Deming rejected the view that the functions of cities were exclusively or even largely administrative. City governments made many decisions that affected the vital interests of their citizens. These were policy decisions, political. Those who emphasized the administrative and business aspects of city government implied that the state should make policies for the city. "The truth is that city government in its essential nature is government; as much so as a state government or the national government and, like them, its conduct is a public, not a private matter."[25] The people of a city were then as much entitled to determine their local public policy as the people of the state and the nation were to determine state and national policies.

The city needed nothing from the state except ade-

quate authority to perform functions of local government. "The state's necessary connection with the city
begins and ends with the grant of power." That the
city was physically located within the state should not
make any difference. The American federal system
afforded an "informing illustration" in this respect. The
states were located within the territorial confines of the
nation. This did not prevent them from exercising their
authority in their proper functional domain. Within the
city all governments—federal, state and local—could
exercise their respective powers. Their jurisdictions, asserted Deming, were "entirely separate and distinct."
The state should pass only general laws applicable
throughout its territory. It should not encroach upon
matters of purely local policy. Once again the federal
experience showed the way. In cases of concurrent
jurisdiction, a federal law superseded a state law only
insofar as Congress had declared a policy. The state
and the city had both a valid interest in functions such
as education, health, sanitation, the preservation of
peace. But it would be improper for the state to interfere, let us say, with a city's conduct of sanitation if
the latter followed higher standards than those prescribed by the state.

The city might in certain matters act as an administrative agent of the state and, as such, would be appropriately subject to the latter's supervision and control.
But, like many of his contemporaries, Deming insisted
that such control should be administrative and not
legislative. Furthermore, the state should never require
a city to enforce a law that happened to be repugnant
to the people of that city. Entrusting the enforcement
of a law to an actively hostile agent was a self-defeating
procedure. It would also embarrass city officials with
their constituents.

Deming would eliminate state political control over
local government. The city must not be regarded as a

"serf" or as a "subject province or dependency," but rather as a self-governing community entitled to undertake all those governmental functions that the local public interests might require. "Thus a city instead of possessing only enumerated powers would be presumed to have all the powers requisite to perform the functions of government within its appropriate field and something in the state constitution or in a general state law would have to be found in order to overcome this presumption."[26]

Deming would reverse the existing rule of law that a city might do only that which it was specifically permitted to do. The concept that the city was a mere creature of the state, subject to the "changing moods" of a state legislature, must be discarded. It was not only unsound in theory, it had been a "prolific source of every variety of bad city government" in this country. It threatened the American way of government, for "genuine local self-government is the ultimate foundation upon which the entire super-structure of our political institutions must rest."[27]

Another notable municipal reformer, Frederick C. Howe, a scholar and a public servant, vigorously supported the movement for municipal home rule. The city, he pleaded, "should be an almost independent agency like the state and the nation." It should be free to frame and alter its form of government, to determine the size of its establishment and its personnel procedures, to undertake any business activity that its people might desire. "It should decide how it shall secure its revenues and how it shall spend them. . . . The city should be sovereign in its own field of action. And that field is for the most part easily determined."[28] Like Deming, Howe maintained that cities should have all power necessary to promote the welfare of their citizens. Instead of having specifically enumerated functions, they should have a general power to govern limited only by the state constitution and general laws.

While Deming and Howe believe that the individual would profit from the instructive experience of participation in public affairs, they are not concerned primarily with his right to self-determination. They are rather interested in making city government more efficient. The city's excessive dependence upon the state—sometime for even such mundane matters as hiring a stenographer, granting leave of absence to a police officer, or banishing chickens, dogs and other noise-making animals from the city—has caused the worst failures in city government. Howe blamed the laissez faire doctrine for the weakness of American local government. Under its influence the people had limited the powers of state legislatures which in turn had slashed the powers of cities. These limitations upon government were imposed "when we were a rural people." But the laissez faire philosophy did not suit the new city which must provide for large aggregations of people and contend with the conditions of a highly complex life, machine industry, and powerful corporations.[29]

It is true that Deming, Howe, and a few other writers did occasionally refer to the "sovereign" individual's right to self-government, but it should be emphasized that this aspect of the case for home rule was over-shadowed by the reformers' concern with governmental efficiency, effectiveness, and honesty—honesty not so much because it was intrinsically good, but because it was the "best policy"; without it efficiency and economy would be unobtainable. The state legislature should not legislate for the city because it was *unfit* to decide questions affecting city dwellers. It was dominated by rural interests who disliked city people and did not understand their problems. Furthermore, by taking on the task of supervising and controlling cities, legislatures imposed upon themselves an impossible span of control. Even with the best of will, they could not deal with the hundreds of local government questions that came to them. Consequently, their performance was poor. Bewildered by the sheer immensity of their task, weakened by constitutional limitations upon their power, they were seduced by evil doers—"spoilsmen" and "robber barons." They had permitted cities to be plundered by vested interests. The cities must be delivered of these legislators, who were at once indifferent, incompetent, and corrupt.

In this century, the argument for local self-government in terms of natural rights and sovereignty has generally been ignored. A few relatively recent examples of it, noteworthy because they are rare, are mentioned below. In his last book, *The Growth and Decadence of Constitutional Government* (1930), J. Allen Smith, a firm Jeffersonian, opposed state encroachment upon local government, saying that while the state was a purely "arbitrary" organization, the city was a "natural and organic unit with interests of its own."[30]

In 1941, Barnet Hodes, the Corporation Counsel of Chicago, observed that constitutional home rule could not ensure local autonomy, because it did not solve the vexing problem of identifying "exclusively local" functions. It might be more helpful to resort to "some form of triple sovereignty."[31] This was not a drastic proposal, according to Hodes; a system of dual sovereignty, created by the Federal Constitution, had already worked.

Writing in the *National Municipal Review* in 1949, William F. Devin, then mayor of Seattle, complained that a theory of legislative supremacy had supplanted "the inherent right of local self-government which prevailed in colonial times."[32] Since the Founding Fathers had based their concept of freedom "upon the doctrine of the sovereignty and dignity of the individual,"[33] Devin challenged the "false" order of precedence that

placed the federal and the state governments higher
than local government. The people were the source of
all power. No recipient of the people's power could be
higher in status than the people themselves.

> Therefore, the closer the power is to the source,
> the higher will that power be. Now with that
> formula, where are the levels of government?
> First comes municipal, for that is close and re-
> sponsive to the people; next comes the state; and
> finally the federal government with only those
> powers expressly granted to it.[34]

Devin would not make the cities into "independent
kingdoms," but he saw no reason why they should have
to go to the state legislatures, hat in hand, and "plead
in suppliant tones."

In the state legislative control over cities Rodney L.
Mott saw a device that would surely destroy the "grass
roots of democracy." Americans must organize a political force to protect the "rights" of cities, but, more
importantly, they must revolutionize their political
thinking. Mott maintained that cities ought to be regarded as equals, not creatures, of the states. City-state
relations should be constituted as a federal system. "If
the federal principle is useful for the nation, why
should not a similar relationship between cities and the
state be desirable?"[35] The case for local federalism
was even stronger than that for national federalism.
Local officials were close to the people, more amenable
to their control than the officials of the "distant" state
government. The proposed scheme would not destroy
the states. Their powers and functions could be enumerated in constitutions. This should be no more difficult than specifying the powers of local government,
which the states did all too frequently.

A federal system would protect the cities much better than home rule ever could. For home rule, even at

its best, represented a grant of powers and privileges from a superior to an inferior. Local federalism, by contrast, would recognize the cities as "political equals of the state."[36] While federalism would not absolutely preclude encroachments by one government upon the domain of the other, it had been "more protective of the states than home rule is of the cities." Mott concluded his essay by saying: "It is time to recognize that our cities have come of age, that they are equal partners in the gigantic business of government in America, and that our democratic institutions can be strong only if our local communities are given full responsibility for managing their own affairs."[37]

The proposition that self-governing localities are the citadels and schools of democracy has always had many adherents. The following statement of an advisory committee of the Commission on Intergovernmental Relations is representative of this argument:

> Local governments are to total government what basic tissues are to the human body. Without them, government would have no vitality. The counties, cities, towns, villages, and boroughs serve as training schools for the leaders of government, and in the affairs of local government are tried those who aspire to State and National office. More important still *is the use of local government to soften the impact of arbitrary State and National laws and regulations and to modify them to fit a population quite diverse in its cultural, economic, geographic, and political elements.*[38] (Italics supplied)

Moreover, municipalities desired to be free to handle their own affairs just as the states wanted to be free from "federal dictation and domination." Governmental decentralization would not be accomplished by placing with the states powers and functions now rest-ing with the federal government. It would be attained only "when as many powers and financial resources as possible are returned to the local governments *where every citizen has a chance to exercise his will directly.*"[39]

The argument for home rule did not go unchallenged. Prominent among opponents were professional scholars, especially professors of political science. Some, though not all, argued that the residents of large American cities, due mainly to the great influx of immigrants from Southern and Eastern Europe, were unfit for self-government. Moreover, the congestion, poverty, and rapid pace of life in the city disrupted the peace and quiet necessary for deliberating public policy questions. In an 1896 doctoral dissertation written at Columbia, where Lieber and Burgess had expounded the virtues of the Teutonic races, Delos F. Wilcox wrote: "The crowded condition, the high cost of living, the extreme development of pleasure-giving institutions, the very noise on the pavement, all unite to destroy or prevent the habit of reflection in the people."[40]

Many opponents of municipal home rule maintained that local autonomy would create an intolerable situation—an *imperium in imperio.* It would destroy the state's essential unity, integrity, and sovereignty. Francis Lieber taught that "a city government is not and ought not to be like a general, legislating government."[41] Wilcox maintained that the city could not be treated "as an independent or semi-independent political unit. It must keep its place as a subordinate part of the all-embracing state."[42] It was illogical even to study city government separately and independently from that of the state, for "government, like the state, must be ultimately a unit." Charles A. Beard denied that there could be such a thing as "municipal science" because "there is hardly a problem of municipal government that is not vitally connected with the wider problems

of state government."[43] The tendency of modern times
was away from the autonomy that cities in the Middle
Ages had enjoyed.

The premise that the state was an indivisible unity
yielded two major conclusions: no functions whatever
could be designated as "purely local"; and while local
"self-administration" might be recommended to en-
hance over-all governmental efficiency, local self-government was a contradiction in terms. Frank J. Goodnow was the foremost proponent of this point of view.

Goodnow felt that the concept of municipal home
rule was medieval. From the seventeenth century on-
ward, the state in Western Europe had increasingly assumed the functions that cities once claimed as theirs.
Such functions as they still performed they did as
agents of the state subject to its supervision and control. At any given time, certain governmental functions
might conceivably be of interest only to a city and not
to the state at large. Home rule, if at all desirable,
could logically apply only to such functions. However,
the state might subsequently acquire an interest in these
functions "on account of a change in the social and
economic conditions of the country." For example,
during much of the nineteenth century, water supply
was an exclusively local problem. But due to the immense increase in urban population, large cities often
had to get water from distant sources. Their water
problem was then no longer exclusively theirs.

On account of the fact that functions which appear now to be municipal may in the future become of interest to the state as whole, it is absolutely necessary that the state, in whose limits the
cities are to be found, shall reserve to itself the
power of taking into its own administration, or
subjecting to its control, any function of city gov-

ernment whose influence has, on account of the
change in social conditions, come to transcend the
limits of a particular city.[44]

What was then the meaning of home rule? Goodnow
observed that it had an Anglo-American meaning and
a European meaning. In the Anglo-American conception, cities might be granted the privilege of choosing
their local officials. It did not include, except until very
recently, the additional power to determine local public policy. That was made by the state. The Anglo-
American system dictated extreme centralization in
legislation and decentralization in implementing state
policy. The functions of local government were enumerated, the rule of law being that a local authority
must show some legislative authorization to justify the
exercise of a governmental power. As a result, state
legislatures passed an enormous amount of special legislation relating to cities. Despite constitutional prohibi-
tion of special legislation, state legislatures continued to
pass it, using the device of classification which the
courts had recognized and approved. Where state constitutions had granted cities the right to determine local policies, the courts had nullified it by unfavorable
interpretation. Home rule had in effect given American
cities little more than the power to regulate, free from
state interference, "matters which may be classed under the general head of local improvements."

The European system of "home rule" empowered
the municipal council to determine local policy, treating a municipal corporation as an authority of general,
not enumerated, powers. The city might do all that it
was not forbidden to do by state law. There was no
need here for special legislation. This did not mean that
in Europe the locality was an *imperium in imperio*.
While a municipality might do whatever the state itself
could do, it did what it did under the supervision and

control of appropriate state administrative departments, which determined also the scope and methods of their control.

> The legislative decentralization, which is characteristic of this method of solving the question, is accompanied by an administrative centralization. In accordance with the principles of this administrative centralization, the actions of municipal corporations, whether these actions are regarded as affecting the interests of the state as a whole or as affecting merely the interests of the municipality, are subjected to an administrative control on the part of the state. By means of the exercise of this control, it is possible for the central government of the state to prevent the municipality from taking action which would be inconsistent with the general policy of the state government, or which, in the opinion of the state government, would be inexpedient for the municipality itself.[45]

The field of activity of European cities, Goodnow found, was much larger than that of American cities. The continental method of granting cities "reasonable home rule" was therefore preferable to the American system. Furthermore, administrative control was "less liable to be influenced by partisan political considerations."

Goodnow reiterated the above thesis in his *Municipal Problems* (1911). His position is especially striking because he was one of the leading municipal reformers of his day, active in the National Municipal League and a member of the committee that drafted the first Municipal Program. This program, it should be noted, endorsed municipal home rule. A superficial reading of his writings might even leave the impression that he favored local autonomy. Here and there one finds him asserting that a city is not merely an agent of the state but also an "organ" for the satisfaction of local needs. For performing the latter function it should be autonomous. He pleaded for the development of a "large sphere of municipal action in which the cities may move free from legislative interference." It was a matter of the greatest importance "to preserve as free as possible from encroachment the city's freedom of action." But there can be no doubt that in advocating local autonomy, Goodnow wanted only to rid the cities of state *legislative* interference. He had no desire to establish that "monstrosity"—an *imperium in imperio*. Throughout his writings he upheld the idea of state administrative control over local government. He felt also that as far as possible the city should not be made to act as an agent of the state. The state should look after its interests through its own agencies. He seems to have thought—as did Lieber, Beard, Wilcox, and Munro—that the prevailing American view of the city as a body politic was outmoded. He wrote, "If we change our point of view, if we consider the city not as an organism complete in itself, but as merely a member of a much larger organism . . . a new line of investigation will have been undertaken from which much good may result."[46]

In his book, *The Government of American Cities* (1913), William B. Munro took very much the same position as Goodnow had taken a few years earlier. He viewed the home rule movement as a protest against state interference with local government. Some of this interference, he thought, had been unwarranted, even harmful. But he would not endorse the "dogma of political laissez-faire." In many cases, state legislatures had intervened for excellent reasons. Home rule, he objected, would give municipalities undue freedom in determining things which, though of paramount interest to them, were also of great concern to the whole state.[47] At any rate, he preferred state administrative to legislative control over cities. Administrative control would do away with that "factious interference with local autonomy which we call legislative supervision."[48]

The case for state control, according to both Munro and Goodnow, was unimpeachable. Where necessary, especially with reference to metropolitan cities, the state should not hesitate to take over the administration of functions which, though previously "local," were now of metropolitan concern. The plea that cities should have a general power to govern and that they should be subject to state administrative, not legislative, control gained widespread acceptance among Goodnow's contemporaries. It found its way into the Municipal Program of the National Municipal League. Practically every standard book on local government written between 1905 and 1915 was a book on comparative local government, giving extensive coverage to local government in Western Europe and lauding the European system of administrative control.

Not all those who have studied how cities in Europe are governed will accept the view that the European system of "home rule" allows greater freedom of action to cities than does the Anglo-Saxon system. It may not even be at all appropriate to speak of self-government with reference to, let us say, French cities. (Paris was Goodnow's model for reorganizing the government of American metropolitan cities.) The "government" of a French city is an organ of the State, the city's role as an agent of the central government being much more pronounced than its position as a body politic. The central government wields extensive administrative control over local authorities. Appointments to certain local offices, e.g., the secretary of the *mairie,* must be approved by the prefect, who is the chief agent of the central government at the "department." He can suspend a mayor from office for one month. The Minister of Interior can suspend a mayor for four months or even dismiss him. The central government can dismiss the entire *conseil municipal*. All of its decisions must be submitted to the prefect and remain on his desk for a period of time before they can be implemented. Needless to say, the prefect may veto a decision for one or another of a variety of reasons. He can instruct a local authority to include certain expenditures in its budget. The whole budget must be submitted to him or to a higher official in the central government, depending upon how large the city is, for approval. There are many other prohibitions, vetoes and controls to which French cities are subject. Brian Chapman, a noted scholar of French local and regional administration, observes that "if comparisons must be made it is more satisfactory to compare modern French local administration with mediaeval England."[49] It would seem that Goodnow's great enthusiasm for the European system of administrative control of local authorities may well have been a case of the grass on the neighbor's yard looking greener. It is likely also that in their preoccupation with administration, he and those of his contemporaries who shared his view underrated the political aspect of government.

CHAPTER 5

Community and Government

More and more in the twentieth century, writers on local government have moved away from governmental atomism. They tend to discard the notion that the weaker the government the securer the citizen. They are concerned with the individual's claims upon government, not so much with his rights against it. The needs of the people become the subject of their theories. Like the proponents of popular sovereignty before them, these writers hold government responsible for advancing positively the welfare of the people. As the socialist, pragmatist, and some conservative theorists had done earlier (and are still doing), they direct their attention to the community where the individual's needs are met. Only genuine communities are entitled to have governments, they think. Some writers insist that the right to participate in one's government is inferior in status to other values in the nation's political tradition: justice, civilization of the individual, and the instrumental values of discussion and debate. Only govern-

ments with large territorial jurisdictions can promote
these values. Like Calhoun, Burgess, and American
Spencerians, some local government theorists relate the
right of self-government to political capacity. Power,
they assert, will not obey any doctrine of presumed
rights. The people will not suffer the power of man
over man to remain with agencies that do not meet the
people's needs, or with rulers who refuse to rule. The
sovereignty of the individual must give way to the sovereignty of the people as a whole. The sovereignty of
the whole tends to remain a whole; it abhors its own
division. Functions of government are then a seamless
web that cannot be divided. The "people" are now
coterminous with the nation, and they have indeed only
one government of which the federal, state, and local
governments are merely the "extensions."

The American city's quest for freedom from state
interference continues, along with the state's insistence
on treating the city as its "creature." As recently as
1959, the City Council of New York resolved to in-
vestigate the possibility of the City's secession from
the state and its establishment as the fifty-first state
in the Union. Two years later, the Governor of Rhode
Island proposed to take his state "out of the nineteenth
century" by abolishing all local governments.[1] Yet it
would seem that by the mid-1930s the home rule
movement had already begun to decline. In December
1935, the *National Municipal Review* announced the
"almost complete disappearance" of home rule as an
issue in American state politics. "Where are the in-
vectives," its editors asked, "that formerly flew at the
heads of those who would dare presume to trample
upon the rights of self-government?"[2] The time had
come, they said, to enquire where the boundaries of
home rule lay. Did the citizens of Rhode Island, for
instance, need institutions of local government at all?
Did the people of Delaware have good reason to cru-

sade against state encroachment upon local rights? Observing that the average American's outlook had broadened, the *Review* urged the extension of home rule beyond the individual's immediate locality.[3]

At the turn of the century, several American writers took note of the emerging metropolis. In 1897 Wilcox cautioned that the growth of suburbs around the cities would stifle the latter's growth. He thought that the state should assume all those local government functions which had ceased to be "purely local." The exact sphere of local government must change periodically, depending upon the "caprice of time, place, and the public will." Furthermore, with the progress of national integration, there would be an "inevitable and resistless" tendency towards central control of local authorities. A governmental function that first emerged at the local level would, as interest in it awakened, expand territorially and become the responsibility of the state.[4]

Goodnow believed that the state must control governments in a metropolitan area more extensively than it did the units of local government elsewhere. He would have the American metropolis follow the Paris model of organization. The government of Paris operated under the close supervision of the French central government. For purposes of administration, the city was divided into a number of "sub-municipalities" (*arrondissements*). The departments of the main city government maintained field offices in each arrondissement, located in one large *mairie* building. Citizens could report births and deaths, get married, pay taxes, register for the draft, buy municipal bonds, apply for minor licenses and transact other kinds of business here. Rarely would they have to go to the prefectural headquarters at the Hotel de Ville. This type of administratively decentralized system, Goodnow thought, would suit American metropolitan cities, especially because it would help cultivate the neighborhood spirit so essential to good local government and so lacking in these cities. It would also bring government closer home to the people![5]

In 1913, William B. Munro saw additional reasons for state interference with local governments in a metropolitan area. Permitting all these governments to make their own independent arrangements with, let us say, public utility companies would inaugurate "a regime of franchise chaos." If the municipalities concerned were unwilling "to be federated into a single unit," the state must supervise the performance of all functions of common interest to the whole metropolitan area.[6] In 1923 Munro declared that a metropolitan economic community had come into being, and that it called for metropolitan governmental integration. He described the "chaos" of metropolitan government in a pungent way, employing metaphor ("mosaic," "crazy quilt") which has since become standard terminology in writings on metropolitan government and politics. Trying to avoid the inconveniences of downtown location without losing access to its advantages, Americans in large numbers were moving out to the suburbs. A "mosaic" of varied communities was forming around the core city. But in spite of this "crazy quilt" of separate municipalities, the metropolitan area was a single economic unit.

> So we have economic unity and political disintegration. . . . The social and economic homogeneity of the whole area results in the creation of problems of a metropolitan character with which the separate municipalities are quite incompetent to grapple. . . . The multiplicity of local governments, operating in the same area, makes for procrastination and waste. Local jealousies retard progress in matters which concern them all. The interests of the whole are sacrificed to the selfish-

ness of the parts. Out of all this is sure to arise, in
due course, some movement for unification, complete or partial, such as will ensure the broad
treatment of metropolitan problems by a centralized authority.[7]

In 1930 Paul Studenski described the localities in a
metropolitan area as parts of a "living organism," and
asserted that the ills of any one of them affected ad-
versely the entire "metropolitan community."

If a section is badly policed and criminality, gam-
bling, and vice are tolerated, if unsafe construction is permitted, if conditions dangerous to health
are allowed to exist, that section becomes a men-
ace to the peace, safety, and health of the entire
metropolitan region. If the streets in a section are
narrow, ill–connected and badly paved, the metropolitan traffic which has to flow through them is
interfered with, to the detriment of all. In short,
backward conditions in one section injure every
other section.[8]

Some ten years later, Victor Jones presented the same
argument. The essential characteristics of municipal
corporations had developed, he wrote, during the early
period of Western technology, during the time of village economy or during the transition from village to
town economy. Consequently, the average municipality
today could efficiently serve only a small and distinct
town. It could not cope with the existing and emerging
governmental problems of a metropolitan area, whose
inhabitants, in spite of a plethora of local governments,
"make up a single metropolitan community." With re-
gret implicit, Jones noted that the metropolitan community was not organized as a unit of government.[9]

While Wilcox, Goodnow, and Munro looked to the
state for solving the metropolitan problem, some other

writers proposed a radically different remedy. In 1915
Robert Brooks urged that metropolitan cities like New
York, Philadelphia, and Chicago be made into autonomous city-states. As compared with the metropolis, the existing state had declined sharply. The budget
of New York City was, for instance, several times as
large as that of New York State. There was then a certain "air of unreality, of the ludicrous even," in the
continued subordination of the city to the state.[10] Besides, the caliber of state governments was low. In an
age of increasing urbanization, state capitols remained
merely "glorified county courthouses." Brooks thought
that in the foreseeable future metropolitan cities would
have to regulate, and possibly operate, many public
service enterprises. They would also have to undertake
large sanitation projects and city planning with the
state's permission. This permission the rural dominated
state legislature would most likely deny.

It followed, then, that state administrative control
would not ameliorate the problem of government in
metropolitan areas. State officials might give useful
advice to second or third class municipalities, but they
would have little to offer cities like New York, Philadelphia, and Chicago, whose own expertise was vastly
superior to that of their respective states.[11] Home rule
did not go far enough. While the exact extent of freedom that it afforded cities might be disputed, there was
no doubt that it stopped short of the state's police
power and its power to regulate local finances, schools,
and elections. Then, Brooks asked:

> Of what advantage to the municipality is the right
> to make its own charter if the legislature can still
> control its finances or impose upon it unenforce-
> able and graft-breeding excise laws. . . . What
> better solution can be offered? . . . Why should
> we not look forward to the entire separation of

metropolitan cities such as New York, Chicago, and Philadelphia from state ties, and their erection into free city commonwealths within our federal system?[12]

Charles E. Merriam also gave currency to the idea of metropolitan city-states. His arguments were substantially the same as those of Brooks. "The state," he lamented, "will neither rule nor permit anyone else to rule over metropolitan regions." At any rate, it was unreasonable to expect New York to supervise New York City or Illinois to supervise Chicago, "when these cities are half of the supervising body itself." Merriam believed also that the great urban communities would exert a much more effective counterpoise to the "centralizing tendencies" of the federal government than did the enfeebled states.[13]

It should be clear that Merriam and Brooks were not advocating home rule as such. They would confer it upon a whole region while, in the process, denying it to the hundreds of municipalities located in that region. In the 1930s other writers maintained that home rule was a privilege, not a right, and that it belonged only to areas which constituted socioeconomic communities. Writing in the *National Municipal Review,* Carl E. McCombs observed:

A unit of local government should represent more than a mere geographical division of state area. [All] will agree, no doubt, that a unit of local government regardless of the size and location, should represent a group of people which has a community of interest, that is, some social and economic common denominator. They are quite likely to agree that for the community so described there should be one responsible government and not more than one.[14]

At this time, one would occasionally hear even a wholesale condemnation of home rule. In 1934 Kirk H. Porter protested:

> The very implications of the phrase "home rule" spell variation, confusion, independence of action —everything indeed which the student of administration has been working to get away from. If home rule means anything, it means lack of uniformity and a high degree of independence.[15]

Home rule is still a live issue, but the significant thing about the temper of the times is that during the past several decades, scholars, public officials, reformers, and politicians have increasingly asked the question: home rule for whom? They have tended to deny that every incorporated place—regardless of its size, competence, and interrelationships with other incorporated places—is entitled to home rule. More and more, they have adopted the view that home rule is a privilege and not a right. In 1932 Theodore B. Manny, an official in the U. S. Department of Agriculture, summed up the new attitude towards local autonomy:

> Local self-government is considered by many a right and not a privilege but the contrary is more nearly correct. As a privilege, it should . . . be available only to areas whose civic consciousness is quite active, whose economic and social interests are well-unified, and whose economic resources are sufficient to finance effective local self-government without excessive or confiscatory taxation.[16]

Modern theorists do not deny that local autonomy is efficacious or desirable. They claim that many units of local government in this country have ceased to be the socioeconomic communities that they once were.

They are therefore no longer entitled to have governments of their own. This argument is advanced generally in connection with metropolitan government. It is
said that with the rapid advance of urbanization, stimu-
lated by a whole series of technological and industrial
revolutions, a new pattern of human habitation has
emerged. Physical separation of localities from one
another has been obliterated so that one shades into
another. Distance has been conquered so that people
live in one locality and work in another. Basic local
problems in a metropolitan area are so intertwined
that municipal boundary lines have become meaning-
less. These localities all constitute one economic community.

More than a half century ago, this thesis received
a classic statement from the British historian and phi-
losopher, H. G. Wells. Addressing the Fabian Society,
he observed that the existing English municipalities
could not meet the needs of the twentieth century because "their areas of activity are impossibly small."

> These local government areas of today represent
> for the most part what were once distinct, dis-
> tinctly organized, and individualized communities,
> complete minor economic systems. . . . Today, I
> submit, they do not represent communities at all,
> and they become more wasteful and more incon-
> venient with every fresh change in economic
> necessity.[17]

In the old days, the residents of a locality lived in contact with their property and/or work. For practical
purposes, their interests did not go beyond a few miles'
radius. "The wealth of the locality was, roughly speaking, local." But the old relationships of physical prox-
imity and mutual interdependence had disappeared.
The interests of a large part of the urban population
were no longer localized.

A large majority of the more educated, intelligent and active inhabitants [of an average locality] derive their income, spend their energies, and find their absorbing interests outside the locality. They may rent or own houses, but they have no reality of participation and little illusion of participation in any local life. . . . It is not that all these people do not belong to a community but that they belong to a larger community of a new type which your administrators have failed to discover, and which your working theory of local government ignores.[18]

Wells went on to say that it was now quite common for people to live in one area, work in another, and do their shopping in still another. The only way to localize them again was to "expand your areas to their new scale." A radius of four or five miles contained the old community, but within the foreseeable future, a radius of one hundred miles (one hour commuting distance) would mark the maximum of the new community. If units of local government were not enlarged to accommodate the changes, the delocalized citizen would not be induced to interest himself in local politics. These would remain in the hands of small tradesmen and other petty interests.

While small communities were struggling for their very existence, the great "synthetic" communities were going through birth pangs and, upon materializing, would absorb the former. There were some who dreamed "of a beautiful little village community of peasant proprietors . . . beautifully healthy and simple and illiterate and Roman Catholic and *local,* local over the ears. I am afraid the stars in their courses fight against such pink and golden dreams." Wells thought that every improvement in the means of communication and transportation, and in the economy generally, "sucks the ebbing life from your old communities into the veins of the new."[19] Many existing units of local government were too impoverished to perform necessary municipal functions, resulting in a "cruel injustice" to the poor when these places were treated as separate communities. Wells would organize education, transportation, water, sewage, and other public utilities on a large metropolitanwide scale.

> I would suggest that for the regulation of sanitation, education, communications, industrial control, and poor relief, and for the taxation for these purposes, this area should be one, governed by one body, elected by local constituencies that would make its activities independent of imperial politics. I propose that this body should replace your county councils . . . urban and rural district councils, and all the rest of them altogether.[20]

Such a "mammoth municipality" would not only be infinitely more resourceful and efficient than the existing little local governments, but it would also be "grand" enough to revive the dying sentiment of local patriotism.

Since the end of World War II, the advent of the metropolitan community has been announced repeatedly by a cross section of American writers, especially in the pages of the *National Municipal Review*. In February 1948, it noted that "an increasing proportion of our population lives in communities that are out of balance economically and socially in ways that make political orphans of people."[21] In 1958 it congratulated the people of Dade County for defeating a proposed amendment to the County charter which would restrict and weaken the recently established metropolitan government there. "The voters of the Miami area endorsed the idea that a metropolitan community should handle its areawide problems on a unified basis unhampered by petty local jealousies."[22]

Many public officials[23]—Josephy H. Crowley, once the Chief Counsel of Cleveland; George H. Deming, once a senior staff member of the President's Council of Economic Advisors and Director of the Conference on Metropolitan Area Problems; and Kenneth C. Tollenor, at one time Executive Secretary of the Association of Oregon Counties, to mention a few—have argued that home rule, in order to be "meaningful," must belong to the "whole city," to the entire metropolitan community. This thesis was endorsed also by the Commission on Intergovernmental Relations. The Commission criticized the "extremists" who intrepreted home rule as a right of perpetual self-determination and invoked it for opposing needed metropolitan consolidation. "Self-determination in one isolated local unit of a large community often restricts the opportunity for genuine home rule in the whole community."[24]

Among scholars who are also metropolitan reformers, Luther Gulick has addressed himself to the question of home rule in considerable detail. In 1957 he observed that there was now not a single activity or function which could be called "purely local." Then what did home rule mean? Surely we could not permit localities to act, in the name of home rule, in a manner that would prejudice the important interests of their neighbors in a metropolitan area. Nor could we allow them to remain inactive when action was needed, and thus "destroy the possibility of the 'good life,' or the potential progress of the entire region." Home rule meant no more than a locality's right to be consulted and heard before decisions affecting it were made by superior levels of government on matters concerning and affecting the locality. This was a "most valuable" home rule right.

We now recognize that every major local governmental responsibility has broader regional connections and that the local government cannot be given full or final power over such matters. All a home rule government can expect to have is the right to act with respect to *some limited aspects* (Italics in original) of these ramified functions. Home rule consists then in giving to the localities the largest possible "bundle of aspects" *to handle within the framework of state and national or regional policies.* (Italics supplied)[25]

In Gulick's view the locality's right to be heard and consulted would be best exercised at the technical-administrative level. It should be more interested in the administrative plans of higher governments for executing decisions than in the broad political-legislative decisions themselves. Here, in the area of execution, "the more vital home rule concerns emerge." Gulick implied that the average locality in a metropolitan area, being far removed from the status of a community, ought not to concern itself very much with political and legislative decision-making. It should leave these matters to "superior governments" and limit itself to being helpful in the execution of policies which have been made for it. It will be seen that Gulick's position here is substantially the same as that of Goodnow presented in the preceding chapter.

It is noteworthy that in 1875 John Stuart Mill had advanced a similar thesis. "The principal business of the central authority," he wrote, "should be to give instructions; of the local authority to apply them. Power may be localized, but knowledge to be most useful must be centralized."[26] Willoughby shared Mill's view. He thought that in the central government there should be a unit corresponding to every branch of local administration that might have a bearing on the "general

interest." The central unit should collect and dissem-
inate information, bringing the experience of one locality to the notice of others as and when it might be
pertinent. It would make sure also that the localities
were not permitted to prejudice the interests of one
another or violate "those principles . . . of which it is
the duty of the state to maintain a rigid observance."[27]

In 1959 Luther Gulick advanced an interesting theory
of the community in a metropolitan area. The people
here, he said, entertained a loyalty for their neighborhoods and a loyalty for the region. This latter type of
loyalty, or community consciousness, resembled patriotism more than it did the sense of belonging to a neighborhood or a small town. Men were bound together in
economic interdependence and in the common enjoyment of many important services and facilities for
which they had a common need. They did not know
each other individually and personally, but this did not
make their relationship of interdependence and shared
vital interests any less real. The "community," therefore, explained Gulick, was not uni-dimensional.

> Even in its local setting, it is a split-level creature,
> with personal, human relations at one level and
> broad impersonal community consciousness at the
> other. This new way of thinking about the com-
> munity is extraordinarily important. To achieve a
> viable social and political system we need to recog-
> nize, foster and build on both of these founda-
> tions, not just one.[28]

Gulick's recent book, *The Metropolitan Problem and
American Ideas,* explores the subject of the metropolitan community further. The traditional theory of
local government recognized that urban centers were
separated from one another by long distances. Each
urban locality was a highly self-contained, social and
economic community. It acquired an adequate and

balanced system of economic activities and social institutions and formed a "natural organic basis for a unit
of local government."[29] However, the emergence of
metropolitan areas had changed this fundamental fact
behind the original organizational scheme of American
local government so that the localities were now over-
shadowed by the new metropolitan community.

Then should today's localities have a controlling
voice in settling questions of their territorial and functional jurisdictions? No! says Gulick. It is one of the
fundamental American political ideas that when necessary the individual interest should give way to the common interest of the community. Furthermore, in determining the public interest "we do not permit the private
interest most concerned to make the final decision."[30]
The public interest is determined by those who are personally disinterested, although they hear the interests.
It follows that when the "organic community" comprehends many municipalities, none of them can individually and independently determine the "public interest,"
let us say, as to zoning, planning, transportation, and
all those matters which involve a broader constituency.
"The concept of the disinterested determination of the
public interest . . . is certainly a fundamental element
of our law and custom. No less so is the concept that the
constituency responsible for any decision must be broad
enough to submerge *ex parte* determinations and, in
truth, reflect the 'common interest.' "[31]

Writers on metropolitan area problems insist that
the localities in such an area are interdependent. But
they observe also that the residents of these metropolitan areas do not regard themselves as members of a
metropolitan community. In the absence of a general
community consciousness, is it wise, or even expedient,
to attempt to consolidate a metropolitan area into a
political society and to equip it with a metropolitan
government? On this question two views are enter-

tained. Robert C. Wood, for instance, who advocates metropolitan government, cautions nevertheless that since "there does not appear to be any metropolitan community, politically speaking, other than that made by a common concern for transportation . . . it would be a serious mistake to undertake to create a government before the political consciousness exists."[32] Gulick, on the other hand, maintains that community consciousness must follow, rather than precede, metropolitan consolidation. Criticizing the theory and strategy of metropolitan reformers, he writes:

> We sought to consolidate mature political entities by their own volition, when we should have known that this is contrary to the laws of political biology. It is just as silly as asking a chick to go back into its egg. . . . We assumed that we could, by words, call into being a broad metropolitan "community consciousness," forgetting that such a community, to be politically effective, can arise normally only on the foundation of a legal constituency with real work to do.*[33]

Paul Ylvisaker, deliberating the question whether the present day "framers" of metropolitan government

---

* The issue between Wood and Gulick has been debated in recent times in another, and not entirely dissimilar, context: world government. Walter Lippmann and Reinhold Niebuhr have argued that the consciousness of a world community must precede serious attempts to create a world government. "The community cannot be coerced into basic order; the basic order must come from its innate cohesion." (Reinhold Niebuhr, "The Myth of World Government," *The Nation* [March 10, 1946], p. 312.) The proponents of world government assert, as does Gulick in behalf of metropolitan government, that community and government grow together and reinforce each other. Robert M. Hutchins reminds us of the Greek view that law is an educative force. It exerts tremendous influence in behalf of its own acceptance. *The Constitutional Foundations for World Order* (Denver: University of Denver Press, 1947), pp. 105–106.

should heroically attempt the establishment of metropolitan government full-bloom or move towards it
gradually through the functional approach, wonders
aloud "what 1787 might have led to had the Founding
Fathers played it cautiously, merely tinkering with the
system in a 'practical, functional' way."[34]

In summary, the above writers feel that governments
are not created because groups of people have a right
to create them. They are necessitated by and predicated
upon the existence of a community of vital interests
among the people of a given area. Therefore, government ought to correspond to this community of interests both functionally and territorially. American localities were reasonably self-sufficient communities at one
time, but many of them have long since lost that status
and, therefore, the justification for having governments
of their own.

Among the forces which have thus transformed localities are the new means of communication and transportation that have conquered distance and obliterated
it as a separating factor. The system of socioeconomic
interdependence which made the people of a locality
into a community has enlarged itself to a metropolitan
scale. People are now interdependent over a much
larger area. It is not contended that the older system
of interdependence was inclusive or that local self-
sufficiency was ever complete. A system of interdependence obtained at the state level and another at the
national level. Then as now a person might at once
belong to several systems of socioeconomic interdependence. It is conceded that the typical locality in a
metropolitan area may still be a socioeconomic community in some measure. But it has ceased to represent
a community of interests in a number of vitally important
matters, such as adequate and pure water supply, air
pollution control, waste disposal, transportation and
highways, land use planning and zoning, education,

recreation, location and maintenance of residential and industrial-commercial property, etc. The question of interdependence is essentially one of degree. The community of interests in such matters as those mentioned above now embraces the entire metropolitan area. In order to protect and serve this community of interests the metropolitan area ought to have a government of its own.

That the ecomonic interests of the people living in a metropolitan area are indeed interrelated may be conceded. Today an individual may live in one locality, work in another, and shop in still another. A business or industrial enterprise may have its executive establishment in the central city and its factory in a suburban town; in addition, its labor force may come from a number of localities in the metropolitan area. The regulatory and service activities of many municipalities will also affect the fortunes of this enterprise and the people working for it. Nevertheless, the thesis of metropolitan economic interdependence would bear qualification. We have seen that the people of a metropolitan area may not even be aware of their interdependence. At any rate, they do not consider it important enough to react to it positively, to act according to its logic. With reference to such people, it may then be more appropriate to speak of interaction than of interdependence.

In what way is a metropolitan area a social community? Those who claim such a status for it point out that the individual is no longer confined to his own locality for the satisfaction of his social and cultural needs. The automobile enables him to make friends with people living many miles away. He can go to localities other than his own to see movies and plays, to hear music, to visit museums. His children need not go to the local school if he does not like it. It is contended that these developments have materially weakened localities as systems of social interdependence. They have also destroyed local social homogeneity. "While some suburbs still remain cultural islands," so the argument runs, "the majority seem to be coalescing with the central city, their populations almost completely indistinguishable from that of the metropolis at large."[35]

Certain observers challenge the above testimony. Wood, for instance, notes that the forces of metropolitan social absorption are opposed by the forces of segregation in the neighborhood. Urban Americans use political authority, instead of economic isolation, to engender among the people of a locality the "critical sense of separate identity." The same technological forces, which have created the metropolitan system of economic interaction, lend themselves to employment for reestablishing self-contained systems of social interdependence. Through zoning, residential covenants, selective industrial development, taxation, and informal patterns of segregation, residents of a suburb can prevent the influx of people from "undesirable" quarters into their midst. The emergence of a metropolitan economy enables certain localities to maintain their chosen patterns of social and cultural interdependence. "Because they do not have to reproduce all the parts of a self-contained economic system and admit clerks, craftsmen, and laborers within their boundaries, a degree of homogeneity can be achieved that was not possible before."[36]

If Wood is right, then reports about the disappearance of local social communities must at best be half-truths. We have suggested above that the assertion regarding a metropolitan economic community is really normative rather than positive. The same may be said of the thesis that a metropolitan social community has come into being. Perhaps what the metropolitan reformers actually mean is that the existing or emerging local systems of social interdependence are inadequate, unsatisfactory, or "bad." Under their influence, "citi-

zens get *parochial* in their political interest and fall into
a *false loyalty* that impels them to vote for the interest
of their little bailiwick against the pressures of broad
regional needs."[37] (Italics supplied) Wood finds that
the ability and the propensity of the urban American to
choose his combination of public services, cultural and
racial homogeneity, trees and sidewalks (that is, a
place of residence) from a wide range of choices does
not represent the best in the American tradition. It is
selfish. The man who so chooses his community in the
"metropolitan free market" has carried the theory of free
enterprise to the extreme. With him, self-interest "becomes the definition of freedom, and issues of equity
and humanitarianism are muted."[38]

There is merit in the thesis that government should
territorially coincide with the community of socioeconomic interests among a people, and that its functional jurisdiction should not extend beyond the interests it harbors, but there is a possible weakness in this
argument too. In the United States, improvement in the
means of communication and transportation has enlarged the territorial scale of important socioeconomic
interests, many of which now operate on a nation-wide
basis. Consequently, functions that were once local are
now said to be metropolitan, regional, state and/or
federal. Functions that once belonged to the states have
now become concurrently state and federal or exclusively federal. The forces that engendered these developments have not come to rest; they go on. Is there
then a limit to the desirability of government pursuing
the ever-widening community of interests and embrac-
ing it? Is there a point beyond which the logic of socioeconomic interdependence should not be pushed? In a
very significant way, the peoples of the entire world
are socially and economically interdependent. Does it
follow that we must have a world state?

The original theory of American federalism recognized various levels of socioeconomic interdependence, with corresponding levels of government. Since some of the Founding Fathers foresaw that these levels might subsequently undergo change, they left the door open to future adjustments by giving the nation a "flexible" constitution. But they did not expect that one of the levels would completely devour the other. They assumed that there would be a limit to the logic of interdependence set by the desirability of maintaining distinct and self-governing political societies in the American federal system. The traditional theory of local autonomy likewise postulated that maintaining the separate political identity of localities was an important American purpose against which the claims of interdependence must be judged. Some of the writers considered above would not let these purposes inhibit their pursuit of coincidence between government and the community. In this they would not stop short of the federal government itself. As we shall see later, they argue that functions of government constitute a web which cannot be divided among several levels of government, that in fact there is only one government of the people of the United States, and that this "government" acts at Washington, at the state capitals, and at local courthouses as the occasion and circumstances demand.

CHAPTER 6

Political Virtue in the Good Community

Many localities are said to fail as communities because they are *too small* to perform vital governmental functions economically and efficiently. The *National Municipal Review* wonders "how all these tiny towns will ever be consolidated—as they must be if the problems of suburban life are to be solved economically."[1] Their very existence militates against using the natural resources of an "area" for the benefit of the "entire community."[2] Too narrow to evoke in men the desire to understand and realize the "good life," they are liable also to violate the principle of disinterested determination of the "common interest." As Gulick explained,

> The people who live and work in an urban area have a deep emotional need to have their city stand for something worthwhile in the world and to present to themselves and to mankind a strong physical image of their spiritual ambition in the structure of the city, in its vistas, in its major

squares and monuments. Through these, men venerate the past, remember the achievements of
those who have gone before, reach for the future,
affirm their self-respect and idealism, capture the
stranger within their gates, and commit the rising
generations to the values and mobility of community life.[3]

Furthermore, these local governments cannot provide their citizens with a genuine democratic political
process. This inadequacy is not accidental; it is inherent
in smallness. Jefferson was wrong in thinking that
American political ideals could best be realized in the
ward republics. Madison was closer to the truth in
asserting that in order to have republican, democratic
government, we should seek diversity and not homogeneity, largeness of size in our political societies and
not smallness.

Two groups of writers on local government repudi-
ate Jefferson for different reasons. Municipal reformers,
local officials, and administrators generally deplore the
governmental fragmentation of the metropolis because
it represents "chaos," inefficiency, and political corruption. The reason for all this mischief is that Jefferson's premises concerning the individual, which underlie the theory of American local government, are false.
The individual is not rational, understanding, unselfish,
and interested in public affairs to the extent that he
would have us believe. Consequently, "rascals," not the
"people," rule municipalities.[4]

Richard S. Childs, the "father" of the municipal reform movement, speaks contemptuously of "orators"
who invest the "pee-pul" with "supernatural" virtues.
Should one point out, he complains, that the people
vote a candidate into political office blindly, without
knowing his qualifications, newspaper editors, who may
be just as ignorant, will scream: "Doesn't he trust our

people?"[5] In the pages of the *National Municipal Review,* political apathy is a persistent theme. It is asserted that apathy is not an occasional or accidental phenomenon, that a certain amount of it is inevitable, that the citizens' interest in, and understanding of, government is necessarily limited. While it is conceded that the individual citizen is "the ultimate sovereign authority in our republic," his needs and aspirations the *raison d'être* of government, it is suggested that "His Majesty" is liable to get confused if confronted with too many proposals in the form of a long ballot.[6]

While writers in this group will occasionally plead for greater citizen participation in public affairs and urge every citizen to be "something of a politician" (which means discussing public issues and candidates with his neighbors),[7] their actual concern with politics is marginal. They are not so interested in preserving and promoting the political values of this nation as in advancing the new managerial values of an urban industrialized society. Proudly the *National Municipal Review* proclaims that the city manager form of government "came into being as a result of a demand for business rather than political management of public affairs."[8] Again: "Experiment, progress, efficiency have been the boast of American business. Most of the 800-odd council-manager places in the United States . . . have demonstrated that the same principles pay off in public as well as in private affairs."[9] These writers reject Jefferson because he is in the way, not because they are Madisonians.

Writers in the second group, whose reasoning is essentially the same as that of Madison, are not oblivious to the values of efficiency and economy, but they are concerned with political values such as individual liberty, justice, and the rule of law. They maintain also that the process of discussion and debate preceding decision-making, and not simple majority rule, is the heart and soul of the democratic method. In debate the advocates of various interests express themselves, hear and understand one another's point of view, possibly modify their own positions as a result, and thus arrive at a decision that represents not only the "will of the majority" but in some measure even the views of minorities.

Madison shared with Jefferson his pro-rural biases. He too thought that the larger the proportion of farmers in a society the nobler it would be. But he must concern himself with the realities of the American scene, with societies as they actually existed, and with human nature as it was actually constituted. Whereas Jefferson founded his theory on the "people"—conceived in the abstract as consisting of individuals each of whom was rational, virtuous, kind, considerate, reasonable—Madison took the "faction" as his point of departure. In *The Federalist* No. 10, he defined a "faction" as "a number of citizens, whether amounting to a majority or minority of the whole, who are united and actuated by some common impulse of passion, or of interest, adverse to the rights of other citizens, or to the permanent and aggregate interests of the community." One could conceive of groups whose interests would not conflict with either the rights of others or the larger common interest, but in Madison's view, this possibility must be limited, for he assumed that all groups representing separate and special interests were "factions."

Factionalism inheres in the nature of man and society. It may be conceded that man possesses reason, but his reason operates in the framework of his self-interest and self-love. Interests of men will then often clash. So prone are men to factionalism that when serious differences do not exist among them, they will find "frivolous" and imaginary distinctions to arouse in them "unfriendly passions" and "violent conflicts." Although a homogeneous population with an overriding harmony of interests may exist in a primitive society, diversity of interests is unavoidable in a civilized society. Madison criticized those "theoretic politicians" who hoped that equality of political rights would lead men to "be perfectly equalized and assimilated in their possessions, their opinions, and their passions." In *The Federalist* No. 10, he scorned those who looked for "a Utopia exhibiting a perfect homogeneousness of interests, opinions and feelings nowhere yet found in civilized communities."

A free government, Madison thought, should maintain a balance among the major factions. But in this it must do more than provide an environment of peace and order in which they would bargain with one another. It must use one faction to check and balance the others to mitigate factional influences upon *its own* decision-making. Government should resolve conflicts of interest in society, but in so doing it should "refine and enlarge the public views," not merely mirror them. It should rise above the "temporary or partial" considerations pressed upon it. " 'Divide et impera,' the reprobated axiom of tyranny, is, under certain qualifications, the only policy by which a republic can be administered on just principles."[10]

While a republican government must respect the will of the majority, it must also provide safeguards against majority tyranny. The constitution of the United States sought to protect minorities by creating a system of separation of powers reenforced by checks and balances both at the area and at the capital. The federal and the state governments would check and balance each other while each was itself checked and balanced internally by its own divisions. To safeguard against the danger of majoritarian tyranny, which depended upon the permanence of the majority's organization and interests, Madison maintained that if there were many distinct interests in society, no single interest, or a coalition of interests, would be able to dominate others for any length of time. The larger the society, the less likely the tyranny. It would more probably prevail in small direct democracies. The principles of representative government and federalism both operated against the tyranny of one group over others by enabling government to extend over large areas.

Madison's theory of "extensive republicanism" in *The Federalist* No. 10 led him to denounce local democracy. He lamented "the notorious factions and oppressions which take place in corporate towns limited as the opportunities are, and in little republics when uncontrolled by apprehensions of external danger." In pure democracies, "spectacles of turbulence and contention" were common, and "they have ever been found incompatible with personal security or the rights of property." The smaller the unit of government, the fewer the interests residing in it and the greater the possibility of one lording over others. The contrast between the Jeffersonian and Madisonian positions is stated well by a contemporary writer:

> The Jeffersonian ideal of grass roots democracy stands in direct contrast to the Madisonian concept of extensive republicanism. To Jefferson, republicanism became purer as it came closer to the people. To Madison, it became purer as it was farther removed from the people. To Jefferson, the ward republics embodied the republican ideal in its purest form. To Madison, the ward republics embodied the evils of factionalism in their worst form. To Jefferson, the principal threat to republicanism was the tyranny of arbitrary centralized autocracy. To Madison, the principal threat to republicanism was the tyranny of arbitrary local majorities. To Jefferson, a republic was a system of government which provided for the maximum

participation of the people. For Madison, a republic was a system of government which separated the people from government by means of representation. To Jefferson, direct democracy was the epitome of republicanism and representation a dilution of it. To Madison, representation was the essence of republicanism and direct democracy the antithesis of it.[11]

In a chapter contributed to *Area and Power,* Paul Ylvisaker notes that any scheme of dividing governmental powers should, among other things, express and promote the basic values of society. Its ability to do so is the "ultimate test" of its virtue. He offers a number of criteria for dividing governmental power areally. One of these criteria or "maxims" is that "the component areas [in a system of areally divided power] should be constituted of a sufficient diversity of interests to ensure effective debate within each component and transcending communities of interest among the several components."[12] The requirement of effective debate marks out the minimum dimensions of a government's jurisdiction. Here the search for homogeneity should stop. In serving the three great American values of liberty, equality, and welfare—as they have emerged from the eighteenth, nineteenth and twentieth centuries —debate has a higher status than efficiency, participation, interest or loyalty. There need not be any tension between debate and these other instrumental values. No one has shown conclusively that participation, interest, and loyalty increase where political boundaries coincide with "natural" homogeneous social groupings or economic areas. It may well be that conflict arouses interest and that loyalty, as mentioned earlier, is a product rather than the cause of jurisdictional boundaries. As for efficiency, Ylvisaker suggests that insofar as "the administrative process is linked with the process of policy, and subordinate to it, it contains its own caution that debate and a diversity of interest are among the conditions of its operating success."[13] But even if debate and the other instrumental values are to any extent incompatible, the value of debate is to be preferred. He goes on to say that diversity enables competing groups in society to maintain a political system of "shifting alliances," which makes majorities impermanent and safe.

With both Madison and Ylvisaker, debate is not primarily an exercise in bargaining between interest groups. It is rather the process whereby contending interests are persuaded to be reasonable. Listening to one another, they accommodate any merit expressed in the opposite views. The resulting political decision is not the lowest common denominator of agreement among them, but the truest possible expression of the public interest, determined with such disinterestedness as the process of debate has been able to bring about.

Diversity of interests calls for larger areas than the ones to which Americans have become accustomed, says Ylvisaker. The absence of a "*general* process of government at the metropolitan level is a crucial missing link in the American system of areal division of powers. That such a general process *should* be developed can be deduced from the theoretical framework outlined above."[14] (Italics in original)

Roscoe Martin also rejects the view that little government is more democratic because it is close to the people. He finds that small rural government is a government of men and not of laws, ridden by political bosses who suppress dissidents ruthlessly, even if they are benevolent to their followers. The citizen, apathetic and uninformed, does not consider local government as government at all. Government for him is at the state capital and more especially in Washington.[15] Jeffer-

sonian symbols and phrases continue to sway the minds
of men, but they have little relevance to the conditions
of mid-twentieth century America, which indeed may
be the reason for their continued popularity. "Since
they have little to do with reality, no interest can be in-
jured by protestation of platitude."[16] Commenting upon
the assertion that local government is the training school
for democracy, Martin observes that small government
does not teach the citizen much beyond the village
"pump politics." It imparts to him a "keen sense for
sectional and special interests," and a sense of hostility
towards all government, especially the Government of
the United States. The parochialism taught at the locality
infests the government of the state also. There representatives of small local government in the state legislature make deals, acting more like a "congress of ambassadors" than like a legislature.

In discussing the "dilemmas" of American democracy, Martin points to the "unending contest between
the whole and its parts." Fragmentation of the interest
and resources of the "whole" into thousands of units
damages society, "for it eventuates in the identification
of self-interest with the public interest and in the plead-
ing of a special cause."[17] Little local government cannot take a large view even when the issues themselves
are large. It is therefore wrong to encourage local action
on matters which have more than a local significance.

It is only as rural government is left behind . . .
that the broad point of view necessary to the
resolution of general problems can be expected to
emerge; for the farther government (that is, governmental officials, including elected representatives) is from the grass roots, the broader the
view it is likely to adopt, the more general its concern, and the less strong its marriage to local
loyalties.[18]

Martin does not mention Madison, but his argument clearly bears the latter's imprint.

Robert C. Wood finds that the hundreds of general purpose and functional "monocracies" in a metropolitan area are at once independent (that is, largely free from popular control) and impotent. They lack the capacity to meet effectively the problems confronting them, and they do not provide discussion or debate before making decisions. The present "quiltwork" of local government plays into the hands of groups who wish to maintain their social and cultural homogeneity, and to this end use local political power to exclude from their midst people having different standards. It enables the petty "elites" of the courthouse to rule the locality in the enjoyment of personal power. These are small men occupied with small matters, "oblivious to the issues which attract larger men." Metropolitan reformers should rise above the considerations of functional efficiency that have engaged them to the exclusion of concern with political values and virtue. They should address themselves to "the creation of an areal pattern of divided powers in which systematic restraints truly operate and the decision making process partakes of qualities of debate and compromise."[19]

In Wood's book, *Suburbia*, he offers detailed criticism of the "republic-in-miniature" in terms reminiscent of Tocqueville's comment noted earlier. Here the pressures for conformity produce passive acquiescence rather than free discussion and debate. The majority, convinced of its rightness, is intolerant of minority rights. If the individual is a dissenter, he will have to contend with "intolerable disdain" for his opinion, as if he were living in an "autocratic state."

The little "republic," institutionalizing the "neighborliness of the village," will produce fraternity but not liberty. Now, fraternity is not without its valuable uses. It gives the individual a sense of belonging and a sense

of security and it promotes group unity and harmony.
But it also breeds narrow intolerance and provincial,
clannish exclusiveness. "Privacy cannot be countenanced
in a brotherhood; personal ambitions bow necessarily
to group aims; unanimity becomes essential, for how
else can a fraternity survive?"[20] The fraternity becomes
especially oppressive when it happens also to be the
government.

In short, the fraternal spirit obliterates the vital
American distinction between society and government.
It violates the equally important corollary that government be limited, restrained, and according to law. Private affairs often become a concern of the public and
public affairs are handled as if they were personal matters. Government of the local fraternity becomes informal, irregular, illegal. "Tickets can be fixed, favors
granted, contracts awarded, not because these irregu-
larities will remain hidden but because they are acceptable on the basis of personal esteem."[21] Little government may be good or bad, says Wood, depending on
how good or bad the town is, but it cannot be just. For
how can justice be administered impartially "in an atmosphere of overwhelming intimacy?"

The American political system at national and state
levels makes elaborate arrangements for limiting the
influence of the people on government. These arrangements do not result merely from the prejudices of the
Founding Fathers. They issue from "a realistic view of
human nature and a thoughtful appraisal of the limits
of popular sovereignty if left to function on its own."[22]
Wood reminds us that men conceive the public interest
from different perspectives, that is, through their own
colored glasses. It follows that in a constitutional government, public policy should be "hammered out in the
arena of discussion and debate"; the majority should
always be confronted with an opposition. However,
being a fraternity, seeking as it does homogeneity and

unanimity, the small community has little use for debate
and none for an opposition. The "republic-in-miniature"
ideology insists that all right-thinking men will arrive
at the same decision once they have the facts. Public
discussion in this context is more of a conference than
of a debate, with the dissenter not a "right-thinking"
man.[23]

Following Madison, Wood observes that the essentially undemocratic character of the small community
is inherent in its scale. It does not contain a sufficient
variety of interests, attitudes, and opinions. It cannot
engender discussion which would produce knowledge
and reasonableness. A hopelessly outnumbered minority will not likely advance its case very far. Thus the
small town loses one of the great blessings of democracy: the opportunity to learn better. "In this way the
prime function of minority rights—to provide an opportunity to persuade, to enlighten, to require the majority
to defend its position more adequately, to amend and
qualify—often goes by default. Sensible men hesitate
to stick their necks out when the prospects of success
are dim."[24]

The large "gargantuan" city, by contrast, is nobler
not only on grounds of programmatic effectiveness but
also in terms of American political values. It has its
neighborhoods, but they do not necessarily lead to per-
sonalized government. There are too many diverse elements here to permit personal acquaintance to be the
bond that holds men together. The "rule of law" becomes a necessity. It may not be all-embracing; "fixing"
may occur in a large city also. Yet relations between
the citizen and his government must remain largely
impersonal and formal, since "the fix cannot operate
in the majority of cases, and it cannot operate in the
sense that the community as a whole flaunts its own
regulations."[25] The rule of law is then, even if imper-

fect, as operative and as well established as may generally be found.

In large cities, unanimity, consensus, and popular
sovereignty do not predominate. The multiplicity of
classes, creeds, and races precludes harmony as a way
of life. Conflict is not expected to be abolished. An
"opposition" is always present to force the majority to
explain and defend its position. The ruling group cannot
banish dissenters from the city. On the other hand, the
"people" do not participate in every governmental
decision. They may do no more than indicate the broad
directions of public policy. Public officials, elected and
appointed, bear responsibility for the goodness of the
city's government, but the "light of publicity" which
focuses upon them keeps them on the correct and narrow path of duty.

The large city also provides infinitely greater opportunities for the development of the individual. For
political participation, intimate or limited, there are
parties, associations, and groups of all kinds. Choices
in the economic, social, and cultural realms are likewise
limitless. This abundance of choices, writes Wood, has
a two-fold significance: "It liberates the individual from
his fellows, while it instills an inescapable recognition
of their presence."[26] Consequently, tolerance becomes a
necessity, no longer a matter merely of personal disposition. Even the possibilities of fraternity are not
excluded in the hundreds of neighborhoods, "each
reasonably self-sufficient in a social sense."

These conditions of urbanity are the basic reasons
for supporting the ideal of a single metropolitan
government, and they seem more logically per-
suasive than the customary arguments of efficiency and administrative tidiness. A [metropolitan
government] is likely not only to be better managed in the professional sense but more demo-

cratically managed as well. . . . It would be less
comfortable, perhaps, (after the blending of the
urban and suburban) than the present organization, but it would be more defensible in terms of
the values the nation has accepted.[27]

The theory of political virtue presented above does
not recognize the sovereignty of the individual. Although it is solicitous of his needs and also of his rights,
especially when they are invaded by the ruling majority, the theory implies that the individual is not
necessarily the best judge of his needs. Even in seem-
ingly personal matters—his place of residence, the
choice of schools for his children, his desire to live
among his own kind—he cannot act as he likes. No
one has a right to be clannish, parochial, narrow-
minded, selfish. The above theory is concerned with
civilizing him. It qualifies seriously the sovereignty of
the people also, emphasizing, as it does, justice and
the rule of law. Justice may be said to mean the settlement of claims of right and assertions of obligation
according to the law of the land, which, as in "extreme
democracies," may be identical with the will of the
sovereign. The phrase, "unjust law," would then be a
contradiction in terms. The law of the majority may
annoy minorities, but it cannot be called unjust. Clearly
this is not the meaning attributed to law and justice
by the writers under reference. They would regard a
local law unjust if it excluded certain classes of individuals from the locality or if, let us say, it outlawed
United Nations documents from the public school li-
brary, or if it denied tax exemption to churches whose
officials would not take a loyalty oath. Implicitly they
recognize the existence of a "higher" law, higher than
the will of the people. Government is a provider of
some of the people's needs and in that sense may be
called their "servant." But it is also their protector and

their teacher. The chief purpose of constituting a civil
society is to form a partnership in learning to live a
"good" life. A preference for aristocratic government
inescapably follows from this view.

The foregoing theory is Madisonian, but its source
is also patently Aristotelian. In the *Politics,* the latter
reasoned that the polis is a "whole," having an organic
unity and a purpose, of which the individual is a part.
He is prior to the polis in the order of time. But the
polis, the whole, is prior to him, and transcends him,
in the order of nature.[28] The whole must exist in good
condition so that the parts may exercise any functions
at all. The interest of the polis, therefore, takes precedence over the interests of individuals, including those
of the rulers. "We must not regard a citizen," urges
Aristotle, "as belonging just to himself: we must rather
regard every citizen as belonging to the state."[29] The
purpose of the polis is not merely to enable certain
people to live "on a common site." It is the function
of friendship, and not of the polis, to pursue a common social life. Nor does the polis come into being
only to answer the logic of economic interdependence.

> The conclusion which clearly follows is that any
> polis which is truly so called, and is not merely
> one in name, must devote itself to the end of en-
> couraging goodness. . . . Otherwise, too, law be-
> comes a mere covenant—or (in the phrase of the
> Sophist Lycophron) "a guarantor of men's rights
> against one another"—instead of being, as it
> should be, a rule of life such as will make the
> members of a polis good and just.[30]

Again and again in the *Politics* Aristotle observes that
the grand end of the state is to educate the citizen and
to promote the good life. To this end other considerations, such as the size and population of the polis, are
subordinate.

Aristotle warns that tyranny will result from the "headiest type of democracy." Here the people, not the law, is the final sovereign. Moved by demagogues and "flatterers," it behaves despotically towards the "better class of citizens."[31] Two fundamental rules in extreme forms of democracy are the sovereignty of the majority, and the liberty of the individual. Assuming that justice consists in equality, the democrat identifies with the sovereignty of the masses. He concludes that liberty and equality mean "doing what one likes." Consequently, each man lives for "any end he chances to desire."[32] This, protests Aristotle, is a mean conception of liberty. True liberty lies in living according to law, which is not necessarily the same as the will of the people. The ultimate and true sovereign is law, which is reason freed from passion and self-interest.[33] A law, made by the majority, that robs minorities of their rights is an unjust law. If the majority take over and divide amongst themselves the possessions of the wealthy, would that not be unjust? (The Founding Fathers asked the same question many centuries later.) " 'No, by heaven' (a democrat may reply); 'it has been justly decreed so by the sovereign.' 'But if this is not the extreme of injustice' (we may reply in turn) 'what *is?*' "[34]

CHAPTER 7

The Web of Government

We referred earlier to the charge of incompetence against local government. Another aspect of the competence theory may now be explored. No governmental jurisdiction, it is said, has a right to authority and power. Power has its own laws, one of them being that it "abhors a vacuum." It will be recalled that during the early years of municipal reform many writers—Howe, Wilson, Goodnow, Deming, Munro, among others— explained the existence of the political machine and bossism in terms of this theory. The boss, they argued, had arisen to fill the vacuum created by constitutional limitation and dispersion of state and local governmental power. Wrote Woodrow Wilson: "We necessitated the setting-up outside the government of what we were afraid ourselves to set up inside of it: concentrated power, administrative discipline, the authority to appoint and dismiss."[1] This theory gained currency also with reference to the vanishing rights of the states. It came as an explanation, and also as a justification, of the so-called march of power to Washington. Addressing the Pennsylvania Society on December 12, 1906, Elihu Root observed:

> It is useless for the advocates of states' rights to inveigh against the . . . extension of national authority in the fields of necessary control where the states themselves fail in the performance of their duty. The instinct for self-government among the people of the United States is too strong to permit them long to respect anyone's right to exercise a power which he fails to exercise. The governmental control which they deem just and necessary they will have and if the states fail to furnish it in due measure, sooner or later constructions of the constitution will be found to vest the power where it will be exercised—in the national government.[2]

The state has been the favorite whipping boy of American political scientists for almost a century. John W. Burgess, Simon N. Patten, William Y. Elliott, James T. Young, Roy V. Peel, Charles E. Merriam, Edward S. Corwin, each in his time, complained of the "unnecessary" confusion and waste produced by the presence of the states on the political map of the United States.[3] Writing in 1928, William B. Munro endorsed Root's doctrine. He observed that the states, having failed to meet the nation's socioeconomic needs, were "all but powerless in some of the fields ostensibly reserved to them by our scheme of government." They laid claim to the regulation of child labor, for instance, but they were unable to cope with it. It was "inevitable" that when a social or economic problem became too large or complicated to be handled effectively by the states, the people would have to choose one of these alternatives: they might conclude that nothing could be done and then "bear the evils as best as [they] can";

or they might call upon the federal government to
tackle the problem whether it belonged there or not. A
practical people would doubtless prefer the second
alternative.

> They will continue to prefer it, and no theory of
> division of powers will stand in their way. Jurists
> may sob over the "vanishing rights of the states,"
> but it is a fair guess that these rights will continue
> to dwindle as our problems keep growing in size.
> The steady erosion of state powers is bound to go
> hand in hand with the increasing complexity of our
> economic and social life. Nothing in the realm of
> political philosophy can be more certain than that
> the intrepid rear guards of the states' rights army
> are fighting for a lost cause.[4]

The people of the localities and of the states would
refuse to remain sovereign and miserable!

Condemnation of state governments continues. It is
said that their decline as political societies is well de-
served. Senator Clark of Pennsylvania contemplates
with apparent satisfaction that "if the states cannot be
made effective participants in dealing with metropolitan problems, they can always be by-passed—as they
have been, generally, in such fields as housing and
urban renewal."[5] After calling for a philosophy of
federal-state relations, Governor Herter of Massachusetts postulates that the federal government must
take over functions which the states do not perform
"properly." It must also aid the states in performing
functions which they cannot, because of their financial
inabilities, perform "adequately."[6] Governor Mark O.
Hatfield of Oregon boasts that "one of the enduring
strengths of a federal system is the fact that the political vacuum created by inaction at one level does not
long remain unfilled."[7] Mitchell Sviridoff, a labor leader
from Connecticut, finds that the concept of states'

rights might be a subject for "fascinating speculation," but it is "irrelevant" to the critical problems of the present.[8] In similar vein, the *National Municipal Review* comments upon the "Nature of the Union": "It is elementary that only the strong can cooperate. The weak are destined to be led, driven, or destroyed."[9]

Roscoe Martin notes that in time of distress, cities have traditionally resorted to the states for assistance. But in view both of history and the current emerging urban problems, he doubts the wisdom of their continued reliance upon the states. He advocates greater federal participation in solving urban problems.[10] To Andrew Hacker, "the states and their lawmaking bodies are dying institutions." Through incompetence and failure to do the jobs that they ought to have done, they have steadily lost jurisdiction to the federal government so that now they "may do the administering, but in truth it is Federal policy they are carrying out." Hacker remains undisturbed in contemplating the states' exit from the American political scene.

> There is no law that says that political institutions must be "resurrected" or "invigorated" simply because they have diminished in power or prestige. If other institutions rise to take the place of the state legislatures, or even in time the states themselves, then realism dictates that we close a chapter in our political history and begin another.[11]

The competence theory applies to local government as well. In T. Bergan Manny's view, home rule should be available only to those areas which have the capacity to finance "effective self-government." In 1935 R. L. Carleton took the same position, adding that the state government should absorb all those functions that local governments could no longer perform adequately.[12] In 1940, an official of the Indiana Department of Public Welfare wrote that the outcome of the contest between the centripetal and centrifugal forces would depend upon the "demonstrable capacity or incapacity of each public jurisdiction to do well the task assigned to it."[13] In 1948 Wilson W. Wyatt noted that local government, the "keystone in the arch of democracy," must do its job well, for "it will be respected as the keystone just as long as it deserves to be."[14]

Scholars and reformers have not lagged behind public officials in supporting the theory that power does and should follow competence rather than rights. Luther Gulick, one of the principal proponents of this theory, maintains that home rule municipalities have already lost, through incompetence and incapacity, much of the content of their home rule to higher governments. They will lose it completely in metropolitan areas unless they find a "firm method" of working together to solve pressing regional problems. He urges them to create general regional governments.

> If the localities don't do the job, the state and the federal governments will do it. It has happened in the past and it will happen in the future. We are dealing here with a law of politics. . . . Politics abhors a vacuum; the failure or the inability to function in the face of need shifts the right to act into the hands of others.[15]

Eugene C. Lee complains that we have failed to reformulate our standards as to the kinds of local government to which the theory of home rule should apply in the mid-twentieth century. Home rule, which is essentially a system of divided political power, cannot be sustained unless all centers of power in the system are strong, vigorous, and viable. If one of them is "weak, inefficient, incapable of meeting the real problems of the day . . . this [center] will become weaker and weaker, until finally it disappears from the political map.[16]

A veteran municipal and metropolitan reformer, Thomas H. Reed, has repeatedly endorsed this point of view. Writing in 1950, he observed that "minor" municipalities had neither the energy nor the resources to meet the demands for governmental services in metropolitan areas. The metropolis suffered from "suburbanitis," for which "drastic surgery" was the only "genuine" cure. "Many of the existing organs—cities, counties, towns, and villages—must be removed and the body sewed together again so that it will function successfully."[17] Twelve years later he decried that "strange perversion of the principle of home rule" which conferred immortality upon every municipality "no matter how young or insignificant."[18]

The competence theory considered above takes the discussion of intergovernmental relations out of the traditional framework of rights—natural, moral, constitutional—and places it in the framework of performance and accomplishment. The several levels of government in the United States are seen engaged in a struggle for power and supremacy. Their engagement in this struggle is inevitable, however, following, as it must, the "iron laws" of politics. In the arena of power, success is the predominant criterion of judgment. Given the necessity for performing certain regulatory and service functions, no other rule is relevant to the problem of dividing governmental power and functions. The tendency of the theory is to accept the proposition that the ends sought justify the means adopted. There is also here the suggestion of an Hegelian twist that what is, is good. That a certain development has taken place is by itself sufficient proof of its merit. The hand of history has shaped it in answering the logic of necessity.

The argument so far does not reject outright the doctrine of local autonomy. It is conceded that large competent municipalities may usefully exercise a meas-

ure of autonomy. A more damaging attack on the
traditional American theory of local government de-
velops when the argument goes on to announce that
functions of government constitute a seamless web that
is incapable of division, that America has fully become
a single civil society, and that consequently Americans
now have only one government, appearances and constitutional stipulations to the contrary notwithstanding.

The view that the "web" of government cannot be
divided has commended itself to a variety of writers—
scholars, elected officials, and bureaucrats in various
governments. Thus according to Edward S. Corwin:
"The national government and the states are regarded
as mutually complementary parts of a single governmental mechanism all of whose powers are intended
to realize the current purposes of government according
to their applicability to the problem at hand."[19] John
M. Gaus believes that important problems facing the
national as well as local governments can be solved
only if "the resources of every level of government
operating in a given area are mobilized to supplement
(not supplant) each other."[20] William Anderson observes that those who demand a "return" of functions
from the federal government to the states assume er-
roneously that governmental functions can be divided
tightly between the Union and the states. On the contrary, government deals with human relations and activities "which constitute a web so intricately and
closely woven that to touch a thread at any point is to
be in contact, directly or indirectly, with every other
point in the fabric."[21] Actually, there are no walls of
functional separation between the levels of government
in this country. It is therefore wrong, says Anderson,
to think that a governmental function must belong
either to the federal or to the state governments. In its
various aspects, education is at once a federal, state,

and local function. The same might be said of health, law enforcement, and many other functions.

The foregoing view receives considerable attention from both Paul Ylvisaker and Luther Gulick. Ylvisaker maintains that government at all levels—federal, state, local—ought to be equipped with a "general power to govern," covering the whole range of governmental functions. It should not be confined to a set of enumerated functions which are deemed to constitute its exclusive concern. He notes that since the Civil War this country has tended more and more towards a system of "sharing common powers" and away from the older tradition of exclusive powers. There is logic in this trend, for the legal "fiction" of exclusive allocations of powers "does not accord with the seamless web of governmental operations in our times. It suggests boundaries where there are no boundaries, absolute distinctions where there are only relative ones. The Civil War began an era which, through the Kestenbaum commission, we have finally recognized and sanctioned."[22]

If all governments have, in Ylvisaker's phrase, a "general power to govern," would they not engage in unlimited rivalry and struggle for power with one another, breeding immense overlapping and waste? They cannot all be independent of one another, equal in status, power, and prerogatives. Ylvisaker suggests that a supreme center of power would in time emerge even if one were not formally created or appointed. A system of general governments should provide for certain "processes" to maintain intergovernmental relations in good order: a process of last resort; a process of intergovernmental cooperation; and a process whereby the several governments may act independently and separately as well as in cooperation. It is essential to provide for a process of last resort because intergovernmental disputes will arise and must be settled. The United States Supreme Court has done singularly valuable work over the decades in defining the jurisdiction of the states.[23] But the process of last resort need not always be judicial. It may operate informally, following the dictates of commonsense and practical necessity.

The process of cooperation will utilize the variety of devices which have been developed in the "multiple-government context of the modern democratic state"—grants-in-aid, intergovernmental planning, and consultation. Cooperation will be facilitated by the link that has been forged between functional bureaucracies at different levels of government. It will increase in direct proportion to the degree to which governments possess a general power to govern. The component governments in the proposed order should be able also to maintain a balance of power system which preserves for them a measure of freedom to do things in their own way.

Since a balance of power system is an essential ingredient of the proposed governmental order, it must provide for the role of a "balancer." There must then be three levels of government, not two. Two centers of power can bring into being only a simple balance which is inherently unstable. It will produce perpetual conflict between the levels and their mutual frustration. In the end, it will break down, causing the subordination of one level to the other. It should be noted that Ylvisaker does not expect the levels in his governmental system to enjoy equality of power in relation to one another. In American experience, the "middle level"—the state—has suffered chronically in comparison with the local and central governments, "having neither the attachment of the one nor the prepossessing qualities of the other." Moreover, citizen interest in state governments tends to languish. Their vitality and efficiency drop correspondingly. If and when metropolitan government materializes, the states may have to fight for their very existence.

> In this coming era of the powerful metropolis . . . state governments will come under heavy competitive pressures. Unless . . . they themselves develop as effective general instruments of government, governors will be taking backseats to the new metromayors, legislatures will dance to the pipes of metropolitan political blocs, and the states may well suffer in full the lurking fate of all "middle levels."[24]

With Gulick, as with Anderson and Ylvisaker, although the seamless web of government cannot be unwoven or its constituent elements resurrected as whole self-contained units, the elements themselves, the functions, can be viewed and handled in distinguishable aspects. Far from being a single indivisible unit, a governmental function, such as education or health, is a "bundle of aspects." Individual aspects in this bundle may be, either by nature or for reasons of convenience, federal, state, or local. The actual allocation of a given aspect to one or another "extension" of government will depend upon factors such as tradition, technology, requirements of good administration, and the political constituency required to settle the related issues of policy. Needless to say, in determining the specific federal, state, or local jurisdiction, Gulick would assign responsibility for aspects of functions and not for whole functions.[25]

According to Gulick, the theory of federalism that envisages independent governments, having exclusive functional jurisdictions, is out of date, if not altogether fallacious. Since the people of this country have become a nation, and are conscious of being a nation, they constitute in fact one single political society. Accordingly, they have only one government (which shall

remain nameless!) of which the federal, state, and local governments are merely the "extensions." Gulick
accepts Ylvisaker's view that each extension of government should have a general power to govern. Yet
each must be a "whole," possessing an internal consistency that commends itself to the rational mind. He
is aware that these extensions will not always work in
smooth and constructive cooperation, since organizations endowed with legal recognition develop institu-
tional personalities, tending to engage in a rivalry of
power with one another. However, this rivalry stays
within reasonable bounds in the United States because
the voter is a member of all three constituencies. Furthermore, like-minded professional bureaucrats, who
dominate all extensions of government, exert a unify-
ing influence on intergovernmental relations. Although
a certain amount of rivalry between the extensions of
government may actually be healthy, continuous and
positive cooperation must overshadow such rivalry. It
is true that the extensions were created to work independently, but they must also work together, "for all
extensions of government are working for the same
American people, spread out though we are over a
wide continent."[26] Men who work for these extensions
must coordinate their activities at the "point of impact," or the locality, where the people are. And since
the locality cannot solve its own problems when these
are of a metropolitan dimension, all extensions of government must participate in meeting them.[27]

Gulick does not say specifically that local and state
governments in the United States are, or ought to be,
subordinate to the federal government. At one point in
The Metropolitan Problem and American Ideas, he
notes that the states may actually have a "higher" status than that of the nation with respect to their own
functions. But this statement is of no avail, for in the
thesis that he subsequently advances there are no func-

tions which belong to the states alone. He presents the federal government as the supreme center of governmental power and authority in American society, asserting that in every society there must inevitably be one, and no more than one, ultimate and overriding power to compel and restrain action. He declares that America has become one nation forming a single political constituency; that the federal, state and local governments are all really "extensions" of a single government; and that the federal extension represents a comprehensive constituency while the state and local extensions represent respectively "intermediate" and "limited" constituencies.[28]

The federal government is currently participating in the solution of many urban problems, e.g., highways, railroads and the commuters, air ports, urban renewal, slum clearance and housing, crime prevention, air and water pollution control, allocation of major water supplies, education, and health. Yet Gulick finds that the federal government is hesitant and evasive. Federal officials continue to insist that their involvement in urban-metropolitan problems is of an "emergency," "experimental" or temporary nature. Since the federal government gets most of its revenue from urban areas, it is right and appropriate that it should be concerned with urban problems. This concern, moreover, should be woven into each and every national program. It would not do merely to establish a department of urban affairs in the national government. Every member of the President's cabinet should be mindful of urban areas and their problems. The national government must make, says Gulick, a "strong and continued central commitment" to upgrade urban life.

The important thing is not for the federal government to "take over," but to *go into collaboration as a positive force,* not as a shy and reluctant

dragon. Many aspects of metropolitan problems
are now inescapably national problems. They
should not, and cannot, be ducked by the federal
government in the nostalgic belief that we are still
a rural nation and that the metropolitan phenomenon is a temporary emergency.[29] (Italics in original)

Elements of the thesis presented above have received
endorsement in many quarters. The Commission on
Intergovernmental Relations, while maintaining that
governmental functions can be divided between levels
of government, observes that no division will hold permanently. "Precise divisions of governmental activities
need always to be considered in the light of varied and
shifting circumstances."[30] Activities of the national
government have vastly expanded during recent decades, bringing about "extensive readjustment of National and State responsibilities." Along with these
readjustments, the law of the constitution has changed
so that the federal government cannot today be kept
from participating in a program if it wants to do so.[31]
The Commission advises the federal government not
to expand its functional jurisdiction to the limit of legal
admissibility. It should preserve the American federal
system and, to that end, help maintain the vitality of
state and local governments. However, since we live in
"an age of peril," we must consider a government's
capacity to govern. "Power will not long rest with any
government that cannot or will not make proper use
of it." Addressing both the radical nationalists, who
would abolish federalism to make government more
effective, and the extreme advocates of states' rights,
who accuse the federal government of "paternalism,"
the Commission notes: "The National Government
and the States should be regarded not as competitors
for authority but as two levels of government cooperat-

ing with or complementing each other in meeting the growing demands on both."[32]

Other writers and commentators, interested in local government and in intergovernmental relations, will be found to have subscribed to the above point of view. Commenting upon the "Nature of the Union," the *National Municipal Review* thus explained the growing and complex "web of intergovernmental relations" in this country: "These relationships are a response to the fact that no matter how government may be fractured and parcelled out, on paper, it must achieve some unity and some consistency of purpose and direction if it is to be effective in an interdependent world."[33] Cecil H. Underwood, a moderate advocate of states' rights and at one time Governor of West Virginia, observes that "a clearly defined federal-state-municipal relationship is impossible."[34] No longer independent of one another, governments recognize interdependence as the rule in American federalism. W. Brooke Graves, who claims to have been the first user of the term "intergovernmental relations," notes that while exclusive assignment of responsibilities to levels of government may have been possible in 1787, it can no longer be done, "for two or frequently all three levels are involved in the administration of virtually every important government function."[35]

Local government officials, though jealous of local autonomy, have not lagged behind in paying homage to the theory of "cooperative federalism." Not long ago, Robert F. Wagner, Mayor of New York City, deplored the attempt at any level of government in the United States to shun responsibility for urban problems on the ground that they were the "proper concern" of some other level. These problems, the mayor said, "must be attacked by national policies meshed with local needs, policies developed with the full and un-

grudging cooperation of the national government working with state and local governments."[36] Joseph S.
Clark, United States Senator from Pennsylvania and
a former mayor of Philadelphia, has called for a "deliberate expansion" of federal aid to cities in evolving
a "national federalism."[37] In 1954 Keith L. Seegmiller,
Executive Secretary of the National Association of
County Officials, wrote a trenchant defense of "cooperative federalism." In a letter to the Commission on
Intergovernmental Relations' Advisory Committee on
Local Government, he said:

> Separation of the so-called "levels of government"
> has been overemphasized. Overemphasis of the
> separation has led to confusion, antagonism, and
> conflict in many instances in an area where co-
> operation and interdependence should have been
> the dominant factors. We have frequently acted as
> if we were independent governments rather than
> separate arms of the same general system of gov-
> ernment. . . . We are the same people motivated
> by the same ultimate desires and purposes,
> whether we exert our self-control through the city
> halls, the county court houses, the State capitals
> or the National Government.[38]

This thesis of "cooperative federalism" may be
summed up as follows: The people of the United
States, having become a nation, now constitute a single
political society. The functional division of 1787 between the nation and the states was meaningful at that
time, since the states existed as separate and distinct
political societies while the nation was only in an em-
bryonic stage of development. With the emergence of
the nation in full bloom, the states have ceased to be
separate political societies. The prime justification for

the original functional division has thus disappeared.*
The sovereignty of the states, their rights and prerogatives, and their reserved powers, are now only myths
of dubious practical value. Discerning men know that
these are not to be taken seriously. Even in law the
exclusive rights and powers of the states exist no more.
By contrast, the federal government is the final judge
and arbiter of its own jurisdiction. However, there is
no need to abolish the states, for, as Hamilton once
said, they can be subordinately useful.

What is the identity of this one government which
Americans are alleged to have? It would not do to
retreat into mysticism and say that the federal, state,
and local governments are all "extensions" of a government which remains nameless. Clearly this government
is none other than the Government of the United
States, that is to say, the Federal Government. When
in the name of "cooperative federalism" it is urged
that we should not fuss over states' rights and sovereignty because all governments in this country are
serving the same people, that the important thing is
to serve the people and not *who* serves them, that
functions of government cannot anyhow be divided,
that all governments must be involved in the performance of all important functions, then the phrase "cooperative federalism" must be interpreted as a modern
American euphemism for the unitary state.

A major argument for any federal system is that it
protects not only the rights and privileges of its con-

---

* Note that the postulate that functions of government constitute a "seamless web" and its corollaries—functions cannot
be divided between levels of government and that all levels must
become involved in the performance of all important functions
—can be valid only with reference to a single government governing a single political society. No one will allege that the
functions of the Government of the United Kingdom and those
of the Government of the United States form a seamless web.

stituent members but also the rights and liberties of the ordinary citizen. Federalism curbs the evil propensities of power by dividing it among numerous competing units (and thus weakening it). Those who make this claim accept Acton's maxims that power tends to expand infinitely unless met by superior force, and, secondly, that "among all the causes which degrade and demoralize men, power is the most constant and the most active." Following Acton and Montesquieu, they view federalism as a balance of power mechanism.

Now while the maxims of Acton and Montesquieu are not false, they are only partially true. Franz L. Neumann offers the maxim that "too little power tends to corrupt and absolute lack of power corrupts absolutely."[39] One may recall also Burke's warning that "nothing turns out to be so oppressive and unjust as a feeble government." Hamilton shared Burke's view, as did Howe, Wilson, Goodnow, Deming, and Munro. Although it cannot be said that the maxims of Neumann, Hamilton, and Burke have less merit than those of Acton and Montesquieu, it is clear that writers on the "web of government" and "cooperative federalism" are more interested in the Hamiltonian than in the Actonian insight into the nature of power.

The Actonian emphasis is not entirely absent from statements on "cooperative federalism." We have seen above that a number of writers, while testifying to the decline of the states, advocate the formation of large metropolitan governments equipped with a "general power to govern." They seem to expect that as the states fail to counterpoise the federal government, the large and powerful government of the metropolis will perform that role. If the states escape the fate of the "middle level" and become vigorous centers of power, the metropolis will become the "balancer" of the American system of government. These expectations may materialize, but occasional ability to play one center of power against another to one's own advantage should not be confused with the capacity to act as the balancer. Historically, that role has belonged only to the greatest center of power in a balance of power system.

It may be largely "academic" to speculate how the balance of power in American government will operate when metropolitan governments do emerge, for their emergence does not seem to lie in the near future. In the meantime, the tendency of local officials and spokesmen to embrace the federal government may be no more than an expression of irksomeness with their present overlord, the state, and of their desire to change masters. One is reminded of Machiavelli's acute observation concerning the behavior pattern of small power centers and its consequences.

> And the course of things is such that as soon as a powerful foreigner enters a land, all the less powerful rulers adhere to him, moved by their envy against the one who has been in power over them. This is so true that the foreigner has to take no trouble to win the lesser rulers. . . . He has only to see to it that they do not grasp too much power and too much authority; then with his forces and their favor, he can put down those who are powerful, and remain in every way the master of that land.[40]

We should call attention to the close similarity between the theories presented above and the views of Frank J. Goodnow and some of his contemporaries considered in a previous chapter. That governmental functions cannot be divided because they are a seamless web will be recognized as an adaptation, if not a straight paraphrase, of the old and familiar assertion that there is no such thing as a "purely local" function. In Goodnow's time, the spider at the center of the web was the state government. Now it is the federal government.

The plea that all extensions of government should have a general power to govern is strongly reminiscent of Goodnow's view, shared by many municipal reformers of his day, that American cities, instead of having enumerated functions, should have a general authority to do whatever may be needed under the over-all state administrative supervision and control. "Cooperative federalism" would appear to be a version, perhaps not so self-explanatory, of Goodnow's advocacy of central administrative control of local authorities. Goodnow would replace local self-government with local *self-administration*. Gulick and the other like-minded theorists would substitute self-administration for self-government at the state as well as the local level.

Goodnow was interested in administrative neatness and efficiency, not permitting himself to be encumbered with any great concern with politics and its values. But Gulick is not in that easy and simple position. He wants to discover the "truth" concerning the public interest, to promote disinterestedness and justice, to protect the dissident's right to be heard respectfully and dispassionately. How do these aims square with his theory of the primacy of power and the indivisibility of governmental functions? The political "idealist" would charge that these two emphases in his theory are incompatible. The "realist" would concede that they are difficult to reconcile but add that in practical affairs one cannot ignore either and must do the best one can in reducing the tension between them. There is a dilemma here which probably no one can fully resolve. As Reinhold Niebuhr says, "Politics will, to the end of history, be an area where conscience and power meet . . . and work out their tentative and uneasy compromises."[41]

Gulick and the other writers of his persuasion may not be aware of this dilemma. However, they evidently assume that the existence of a vigorous and effectively organized government, guarding and presiding over a balance of power system in society, is a pre-requisite to the realization of their ideals. Convinced that governmental weakness is a greater threat to liberty than governmental strength, they hope this guardian will not seek, or can be kept from seeking, self-aggrandizement.

CHAPTER 8

Reflections

The theories of local government we have been considering would appear generally to be normative. It will be seen that the appeal of certain writers to history is an act of choice. History is the repository of all kinds of lessons. It is a mistress from whose door no suitor is returned unrewarded. In pointing to certain historical experiences, while ignoring others, theorists of local government have sought to justify their portrayals of the good society. In applying the law to a determination of the rights and privileges of localities, they have chosen certain canons of constitutional interpretation, and rejected others, to accommodate their notions of political and governmental virtue. In exploring the socioeconomic foundations for a governmental order, in examining concepts of the community, they have been guided by their view of the good life. The controversy over local self-government studied in the preceding pages is basically a controversy over values and ideals.

It would be futile to criticize the Jeffersonian argument for local self-government on the ground that its elements—the state of nature, man's possession of divine reason, inherent and inalienable rights, the social contract—are figments of the imagination. Such indeed they may well be. But to this charge they are not uniquely vulnerable, since they are, like the starting premises of many political philosophers, assumptions. Their authors have advanced them in the conviction that men would attain virtue if in the conduct of their affairs they proceeded on the basis of these rather than some other and possibly contrary assumptions. According to the Jeffersonians, political virtue comprehends, besides the protection of one's life and possessions, freedom for the individual to develop his capacities— physical, spiritual, moral, intellectual—to the fullest possible extent. Self-government makes men sturdy, self-reliant and adventurous; even deliberative, considerate, reasonable, and just.

The basic assumptions and the structural design of Jeffersonian theory are incompatible with its ethical goals—justice, and the civilization of the individual. Government is said to be an umpire among men, but its judicial character is vitiated by crowning direct democracy as the apex of republican virtue. Disinterestedness is essential to the judicial function. When judgments upon interests at issue are rendered by the citizens of a ward republic, including those directly involved, the judicial quality of the result is bound to be impaired. Jefferson would have done well to heed Locke's observation that the state of nature had to be terminated because of the "evils which necessarily follow from men's being judges in their own cases." Men are biased, said Locke, in their own favor, and they are ignorant of the law of nature because they do not study it. Furthermore, as Wood has asked, how can justice be rendered in an atmosphere of overwhelming intimacy?

Civilization of the individual through self-government is an ancient ideal. When a man is fully civilized, he may follow his heart's desire without doing wrong, since then his heart does not desire that which it ought not to desire. In the classical explanations of this ideal, self-government means subjecting one's impulses, one's "irascible and concupiscible powers," as Saint Thomas Aquinas put it, to the "royal and politic rule" of reason. In recounting the death of Socrates, Plato provides a perfect illustration of civilization through self-government. Refusing to escape from the prison, Socrates argues:

> The Athenians have thought it fit to condemn me, and accordingly I have thought it better and more right to remain here and undergo my sentence; for I am inclined to think that these muscles and bones of mine would have gone off long ago to Megara or Boeotia . . . if they had been moved only by their own idea of what was best, and if I had not chosen as the better and the nobler part, instead of playing truant and running away, to undergo any punishment which the state inflicts. . . . It may be said, indeed, that without bones and muscles and the other parts of the body I cannot execute my purposes. But to say that I do as I do because of them, and this is the way in which mind acts, and not from choice of the best, is a very careless and idle mode of thinking.[1]

That men should impose upon their impulses and desires the rule of reason may not be denied. But whether participation in the government of the civil society also leads to the individual's civilization is a different and moot question. One may object that such a procedure is like putting the cart before the horse. The individual becomes entitled to participation in the governance of society after he has attained civilization, not as a means of attaining it. Both Locke and Jefferson tell us that the function of government is predominantly judicial. Is it then fair that the rights and liberties of individuals should be passed upon by other individuals as a part of their apprenticeship in self-education?

As Tocqueville observed, the individual, possessed of the notion that he is sovereign, tends to become selfish, self-centered, unmindful of his responsibilities to his fellow men, and apathetic towards the political process. The concept of the individual's sovereignty is subversive of both society and government. In the quest for equality of condition, which is one side of the coin of which the other is his presumed sovereignty, he is likely to foresake self-reliance and welcome authoritarian government that promises to bring about and maintain equality. The companion principles—sovereignty of the people and majority rule—breed among citizens of ward republics intolerance of the rights of minorities.

It is impossible to deduce from the doctrine of the sovereignty of the individual a theory of government in which justice or his civilization is a major concern. This doctrine will yield only one conclusion concerning the nature of government, to wit, that it is a grand piece of conference machinery. Its principal function is to provide facilities for sovereigns (in the ward republics) and their ambassadors (at the state and national levels) to assemble and bargain with one another without resorting to physical violence. The operating principle in concluding bargains at these congresses of sovereigns and diplomatists is power, notwithstanding the condemnation that it is said to merit. For in the final analysis, the force of numbers is merely a substitute for the force of arms. No wonder then that government, conceived as a conference machinery, is intended to be severely limited in size. It would break down if its territorial and/or functional jurisdiction were large.

The emphasis that Cooley and his followers place upon prescription has a familiar Burkean ring, as does their preference for gradualism. They maintain that custom represents the wisdom of the ages which should not be dismissed lightly, for it may be superior to any single individual or group judgment. But the substance of their thesis carries the imprint of Jefferson also. This apparent incompatibility of influences is resolved when we consider that Jeffersonian theory had already become an important part of the American political tradition by the time Cooley wrote. A salute to Jefferson would then be perfectly appropriate for a traditionalist, conservative American.*

It should be noted that conservatism, of which the principle of prescription is a central part, is not an "ideational" philosophy. It does not preach a substantive ideal. No description of the institutions of a conservative "good society" can be given. Conservatism represents rather an attitude towards existing institutions. It is concerned with the process and the rate of change, not with the purpose or direction of change. As Huntington points out, it is not at all strange to find Edmund Burke defending Whig institutions in

* The revolutionary philosophy of Jefferson provides the Cooley school with the substance of its conservative philosophy. But it should be noted that the conservative leaves out the most dynamic element in Jeffersonian theory, to wit, that the reason of the individual, being adequate for dealing with worldly affairs, ought to be the author of governmental decisions. The doctrine of prescription necessarily dethrones the individual's reason and places in its stead human reason—the wisdom of the race. The spirit of the Cooley doctrine would then appear to be anti-Jeffersonian.

England, democratic institutions in America, autocratic institutions in Europe, and the ancient Hindu
institutions in India.[2]

There is merit in the advice that one should approach existing institutions and practices respectfully,
because they may represent the wisdom of the ages,
and that one should alter them, if one must alter them,
deliberately and gradually, not impetuously or radically. But reverence of tradition is not without its draw-
backs. Our definitions of wisdom and folly are subject
to change. The Greek "wisdom" concerning slavery
and the ancient Hindu "wisdom" concerning untouch-
ability are repugnant to the conscience of the modern
man. Their continued existence in parts of the world
today may be said to represent the folly, not wisdom,
of the ages. Now an advocate of prescription may protest that he is not opposed to change, that he only urges
deliberation and gradualism. But how gradual is gradual enough? Since preference for gradualism is essentially an attitude of mind, its dictates in a given situation are bound to be unauthoritative and nebulous. It is
then no accident that conservatives often invoke the
majesty and authority of tradition only to defend the
status quo, and oppose even slight departures from it.
This pitfall Judge Cooley and his followers have not
always avoided in spite of their professions of respect
for claims of due change. Recall, for instance, the case
of *Allor* v. *Wayne County Auditors* (43 Michigan 76,
1880). A metropolitan police force for Detroit existed.
The state legislature, presumably to integrate and
streamline the city's police organization, conferred
upon it the powers that police "constables" had previously held under existing law and custom. Chief Justice
Campbell, Cooley concurring, invalidated the state law
on the ground that ancient custom had fixed the rights
and duties of constables in "our constitutional polity."
Surely the change sought by the state legislature in this

case could not be called radical. Yet the Court disallowed it.

The commitment of Judge Dillon and his adherents to an absolutist concept of state sovereignty follows the mainstream of Western thought on the subject. Like Bodin, Hobbes, Bentham, Austin, Calhoun, Burgess, and Lieber, they conceive of sovereignty as the supreme, absolute, indivisible power in the state. The word of the sovereign is law. The *status quo*—maxims, custom, vested rights—has no special claim upon judicial consideration. The unitary concept of sovereignty persuades the Dillon school to view the "people" as a whole, as an entity, and not as individuals. The sovereignty of the individual may have the sanction of American tradition, but it remains outside the pale of law. If the sovereign authority in the state—the legislature representing the "whole people"—wants to break away from tradition and open new ways of thought and action, judges cannot stand in its way.

The Dillon school mirrors the passage of American political tradition from Madisonian "republicanism" to Jacksonian "democracy," from "conservatism" to "liberalism." Cooley believed in laissez faire, limited government, checks and balances. Judges of the Dillon school partake of the tradition, beginning in their circles with the accession of Chief Justice Taney to the Supreme Court of the United States, that the main business of government is to promote the welfare of the people as defined by their spokesmen in state legislatures. The rise of the theory that localities are the creatures of the state represents the recognition in American law of the rise of the masses to political power and especially of their claim to its fruit.

Modern American theorists seem generally to eschew the philosophy of natural rights; also, they look askance at the doctrine of an inherent right to local self-government. A number of them—Elihu Root,

Judge Timlin, W. B. Munro, Luther Gulick, Andrew Hacker, Senator Clark, Governors Herter and Hatfield, Kirk Porter, Eugene Lee, Wilson Wyatt, R. L. Carleton, among others—maintain that if there is a "right" to power at all, it belongs to those who are fit to possess it because they have the ability to use it. Today the claim of many a locality to self-government is bogus because it is too weak—financially, organizationally, intellectually—to exercise powers of self-government. The weak are not only ineligible to rule, they cannot even cooperate with the powers that be. They are "destined to be led, driven, or destroyed."

The criterion for determining the competence of a local government, and thus the admissibility of its title to self-government, is its success in solving the "problems" that confront it. The theory of power has it that when a subject for the exercise of governmental power arises and the local government concerned fails to apply power to it, either because it is lacking in such power or because it is unwilling to use the same, the subject moves on to other quarters in its desire to embrace power. Power at other centers moves to answer its call. All this happens automatically, as it were, in obedience to the iron laws of power politics. That control over a function has moved away from the jurisdiction of a government is *ipso facto* proof positive that the government concerned was incompetent, and therefore ineligible, to have jurisdiction over this function.

What are the "problems" which a municipality must solve before it may be deemed to have established its claim to competence and, therefore, to self-government? One way of answering these questions would be to hear the testimony of functional experts in various fields, to make an image of the "good society" with their advice, and then to judge the actual performance of a municipality against the criteria so drawn (or overdrawn). Often such a procedure is followed. Alternatively, one may refer to the judgment of history as written in the arena of power politics. The supreme sovereign in society becomes the ultimate judge of these questions and decides, with or without the aid of functional experts, whether various governments have well met the problems that they ought to have met.

The theory of the primacy of power is an ancient one, not a concoction of our writers on local government. "Of the gods we believe," said Thucydides, "and of men we know, that by a necessary law of their nature they rule wherever they can." One may recall also Hobbes's celebrated statement in the *Leviathan:* "I put for a general inclination of all mankind, a perpetual and restless desire for power after power, that ceaseth only in death." Other eminent authorities might be quoted. Nevertheless, in applying the "laws" of power to the study of intergovernmental relations we should remember that the power we speak of is that of man over man. The nature of its laws is therefore no more patent than the nature of factors bearing upon human motivation. Men are moved not only by their desire to solve "problems" but also by their attachment to traditional values. The latter may urge them to ignore, rather than meet, certain problems, even to depart from the scene where these problems rage. Our criticism of the theories of power and competence is not that they are false, but that they are not fully adequate frames of reference for condemning or defending current trends in intergovernmental relations.

The proposition that government is a web and that its functions cannot be divided among levels of government follows readily from the theory of power reviewed above, especially from the thesis that power tends to concentrate at one center and does not suffer its own division. This proposition may be correct, if asserted with reference to the governance of a single civil society. It is no accident, then, that writers who advance this theory in connection with intergovernmental relations maintain that the United States, as a result of technological advances of various kinds, has become a closely knit nation, that is, fully a single civil society. They suggest also that the states and the localities cannot any longer be regarded as separate civil societies. Local, state, and federal governments are really the extensions of a single government, which is the government of the people of America. Since they cannot have their exclusively separate functional jurisdictions, they should all have a general power to govern. They should also have a "process of last resort" to settle their jurisdictional and other disputes. Whichever government presides over this process of last resort is supreme over others. Specifically, the federal government has already achieved this position of supremacy, for it can now determine its jurisdiction, and thus influence the jurisdictions of other governments, by its own action. As noted earlier, the adherents of this theory see the American governmental system tending toward a unitary order.

This raises an interesting question: Can federalism ever endure? Or does the process of its eventual obsolescence begin even while the ground is being prepared for its emergence? Dicey once wrote that a federal government comes into being because the constituent states want "unity" but do not want "union." They share certain important interests. They wish to come closer together and institute agencies for joint action to execute certain common purposes. But the identity of their interests is not extensive or profound enough to outweigh their sense of separateness. During the early years of their association—the "courtship" period, as some call it—they may be fiercely jealous of their independence. As the experience of joint action under common governance proceeds, they will either fall apart and revert to their original status of complete independence or they will begin to merge their separate

identities toward forming a single entity. When the
merger of these separate wills has finally blossomed
into a "union," the federation begins to take on the
character of a unitary state.

It should be noted that several nineteenth century
American political scientists and commentators, who
happened also to be nationalists, asserted that federalism was essentially a transient form of political association. Elisha Mulford thought that in the early stages
of its political development, or in a period of degenera-
tion, a people might constitute a federal system. But
it would have to be a temporary expedient.[3] Entertain-
ing a mystical concept of the nation, he saw an inherent antagonism between nationalism and federalism.
Federations themselves were impermanent, "but the
evil principle, the bite of the serpent, remains, and in
some sudden moment it may rise and strike at the life
of the nation."[4] Mulford objected that federalism represented society merely as an artificial and voluntary
association or partnership in certain interests. "The
confederacy comports only with an extreme individualism—the association of private persons, the accumula-
tion of special interests—to be terminated when these
may dictate or suggest."[5] By contrast, the nation existed
in an organic and moral relation to its members.

Writing in 1890, John W. Burgess observed that
federalism suited states having a large territory in-
habited in its various sections by different ethnic and
nationality groups. With the passage of time, these ethnic and nationality distinctions might well be overcome. In that event, such a state might still retain the
federal form, but its original character would change.
The local governments would become "more and more
administrative bodies, and less and less law-making
bodies." Burgess saw the entire world, including federations, tending towards a "system of centralized government in legislation and federal government in adminis-

tration." This, he thought, was the pattern of the future, "the ultimate, the ideal form, at least for all great states."[6]

The alleged tendency of the United States towards unitarianism is not unique. There is a vital connection between federalism and nation–making. The experience of federations more recent than the United States further illustrates it. Switzerland adopted federalism at a time when the Swiss people were already conscious of being a nation. The federal government there is one of enumerated and delegated powers. Sovereignty belongs to the cantons, which have the residuary powers of government. But the enumerated powers of the federal government have always been extensive, with a general supervisory power over all governmental functions. The cantons have exclusive jurisdiction over none. The federal law "breaks cantonal law," and there is no judicial review to declare that the federal government has usurped cantonal powers. Swiss federalism consists largely in entrusting to the cantons "primary" responsibility in certain matters and in using their governments for executing the federal law.

Discussing the relevance of federalism to Italy, John Stuart Mill stated what may well be the crux of the matter.

The question may present itself (as in Italy at its present uprising) whether a country, which is determined to be united, should form a complete or a merely federal union. . . . The question then is, whether the different parts of the nation required to be governed in a way so essentially different that it is not probable the same Legislature, and the same ministry or administrative body, will give satisfaction to them all. Unless this be the case, which is a question of fact, it is better for them to be completely united. . . .

Whenever it is not deemed necessary to maintain permanently in the different provinces, different systems of jurisprudence, and fundamental institutions grounded on different principles, it is always practicable to reconcile minor diversities with the maintenance of unity of government. All that is needful is to give a sufficiently large sphere of action to the local authorities.[7]

Whether the United States has actually become a single civil society, and whether the states and the localities have ceased to be separate civil societies, may be debatable questions. It is significant, however, that an increasing number of writers assume, and would have their readers believe, that these developments have already come to pass or are in the process of taking place.*

We have seen that certain writers invoke the authority of the laws of power not only to explain but sometime also to justify the movement of governmental power away from the localities to the states and from the states to the federal governent. They do so in the name of social change, since there are new problems and new needs, they say, which must be answered. If one level of government does not answer them, another must and will. Implicit in this reasoning is the assumption that "social change" contains within itself its own defense and justification. Its propriety cannot, or should not, be open to question. Necessities decreed under its authority have a sovereign quality. Government must

---

* It may be interesting to note that as early as 1838, Francis Lieber apparently thought that these developments had materialized. He described the American system as an "hamarchy," that is, a "polity which has an organism, an organic life . . . in which a thousand distinct parts have their independent action, yet are by the general organism united into one whole, into one living system." *Manual of Political Ethics* (Philadelphia: J. B. Lippincott, 1881, first published 1838), I, pp. 353, 355.

heed them. If its existing constitution interferes with its duty to carry out these decrees, then the constitution must change. If in the process, certain political values fall by the wayside, then so be it. The grand ends of governmental endeavor are fixed by the hand of history following the logic of necessity. Now means must be found that are equal to the task.

When we proclaim the departure of the horse-and-buggy age and insist that government must adapt its fundamental principles and structure to the socioeconomic consequences of our modern technology, we might well pause to ask if it would not be appropriate also to guide the movement of technology, to control its "problem-creating" potential in such a way that the governmental order does not have to be altered radically in order to accommodate social change. Let us, for purposes of illustration only, raise the following question: does an auto manufacturer have an unlimited right to build ever larger cars even if they create traffic congestions and parking problems with which many municipalities cannot cope, then seeking solutions elsewhere and changing the American governmental system in the process? Is the right to design the wheel base of a car any more precious than some other aspects of the American political tradition? Another question may be asked, again to illustrate the point. Much of the so-called "march of power" to Washington is justified as an inevitable result of the burdens of world leadership which this country has to bear. But the assumption of these burdens should have been fully an act of deliberate choice. Surely it is not a divine ordinance that Americans be the arbiters of human destiny all over the globe. When such choices are made, their likely consequences at home should also be considered. It would be ironical indeed if any of the values that Americans were defending in the Cold War declined merely as an unintended consequence of certain decisions in foreign policy. It is not suggested that a certain stage in the development of American governmental system is sacrosanct and that there it should be frozen. But it is submitted that change occurs in many ways. Men who preside over a system may change it advisedly, or they may let change come upon them.

Some writers—H. G. Wells, Paul Studenski, Victor Jones, Austin McDonald, Luther Gulick, Robert Wood, Carl McCombs, Eugene Lee, and members of the Commission on Intergovernmental Relations—postulate that the territorial jurisdiction of government should coincide with the area of a fairly self-contained socio-economic community. Such a community may even be said to have a right to self-government. When a locality ceases to be a community, when the social and economic needs of its citizens become intermeshed with similar needs of the citizens of neighboring localities, its government cannot meet these needs adequately. It becomes incompetent, inefficient, wasteful. It begins to harbor a power vacuum that waits to be filled from outside. Its inabilities endanger the prospect of a "good" life for its citizens. It forfeits their loyalty and affection. The quality of its political process declines.

A political theory based upon the primacy of the community does not recognize an unlimited right to self-government. Governments may be formed only for "acceptable" purposes. If each individual had been self-sufficient, society and government might never have arisen. They are founded upon his inadequacy and his dependence, not upon his sovereignty. Society or community, where the interdependence of individuals is recognized and acted upon for the greatest possible satisfaction of the needs of all, is so vital to human well-being that its own existence cannot be regarded as a function of the individual's desire or design. It has a being of its own and may be said to have rights and claims of its own that must be weighed alongside the claims of individuals and groups. The "good of the community" may not be sacrificed to the interests of any individual or group. For the community is a corporate being, whose concerns comprehend the existing and also the coming generations.

The concept of the corporate community is endorsed by many of the writers considered above. The community is described as a "living organism," as a separate "organic socio-economic unit," as a "natural social unit" with its own "spirit" and "ideals." Implicit in this concept is a principle of aristocratic government. Consider the teachings of some of our community theorists: an isolated local unit in a large community should not be allowed to restrict the opportunity for genuine home rule in the whole community; the purposes for which the independence of many a municipality is maintained are unworthy and repugnant to the nobler part of the American tradition; the interest of the individual must give way to the interest of the community when necessary; the private interests most concerned in an issue should not have a controlling voice in settling it; the decision maker ought to be personally disinterested in the issues that come before him; while he should hear the interests pleaded before him, he should also consider the interests that have gone unrepresented, such as the interests of posterity. Government may be the agent of the people, but it is also the agent of the corporate community. It acts as the guardian and the promoter of the community's virtue and wisdom. The purpose of its laws is not merely to announce the decrees of the victor in the arena of power politics or the decisions of a congress of sovereigns. Their purpose, in addition to accommodating the interests of private parties insofar as these can be reconciled with the "public interest," is to educate and civilize the people; to help them understand the meaning of freedom and the responsibility of free men to one another; to help them overcome their selfishness, their narrow parochialism; to lead them to "venerate the past . . . reach for the future, affirm their self-respect and idealism, capture the stranger within their gates"; in short, to guide them toward the "good life."

Some of the above theorists are concerned also with a locality's capacity to attain political virtue for the pursuit of truth and justice: the rule of law; disinterested discovery of the public interest; tolerance of the opponent's view and willingness to learn from him. They contend that smallness of jurisdictional size is inherently hostile to considerations of political virtue while largeness of size is an indispensable condition of attaining it. As with Madison so with Gulick, Wood, Ylvisaker, and Martin, the proliferation of interests in a large territory is a happy circumstance because it not only prevents one interest from over-awing the others but enables the government to balance them all off and to keep any one or a combination of them from overwhelming it.

In this interpretation of political virtue, sovereignty is denied to the individual. It is denied also to his reason, unless that is divorced from his desire, self-interest and self-love. Needless to say, reason so divorced is no longer the reason of a specific individual. It has become the reason of man, the species. Under its guidance, the individual renders a cool and dispassionate judgment upon interests at issue including his own. He has conquered himself. He has become civilized. This would appear to be the significance of the emphasis that authors of this theory place upon discussion and debate. The individual is asked to confront his interests with those of others. He is asked to defend his interests, not like the lawyer whose sole objective is to win his case, but like a seeker of the truth. He is asked to hear others defend their interests not merely to find loopholes in their reasoning with which to embarrass them, but to learn from their exposition and argument, to concede that which is reasonable in their position, and finally to modify his own. In the good society, discussion and debate represent a higher value than the individual's participation in the conduct of government. Democracy, it is said, does not require a one-to-one relationship between electoral participation and policy making.

The proponents of this view remind us that the Founding Fathers placed in the federal constitution a number of elaborate provisions designed specifically to mitigate the influence of the people upon their government. They established a system of representative government. Direct democracy many of them abhorred, not without reason.

The subject of the individual's participation in the governance of society has engaged democratic theorists perennially. During this century, it has been a lively question among American students of local government, metropolitan government, and inter-governmental relations. Faith in the desirability of participation supplies an important objection to metropolitan integration and to the transfer of control over governmental functions from localities to the states and from the states to the federal government. The subject is complex and baffling, especially because the feasibility of participation is not as apparent as its desirability.

Many municipal reformers have sought to maximize the individual's participation in government. After recommending the long ballot and short terms of elective office, they discovered, as some had before them, that the individual was apathetic. Others in turn asserted that the long ballot engendered apathy because it imposed impossible demands upon the individual's time, attention, and comprehension. They in turn advocated the short ballot. Still others found in the over-extension of governmental functions a major reason for apathy. The more optimistic observers concluded that apathy need not perturb us; the people were apathetic because they were content with the *status quo.* Some writers on politics assert that there are many ways of citizen participation in government besides either the town meeting or voting in elections. York Willbern notes that through field administrators of national and state programs "the pulse of the people may go back up [the] hierarchy far enough to register accurately." Then the citizen acts also through many semi-public and private agencies which bring pressure to bear upon government on his behalf: the community chest, the League of Women Voters, the PTA, the chamber of commerce, the labor union, and a host of other clubs, agencies, and organizations. Willbern believes that this type of participation "may well constitute a more active and effective form of self-government than is involved in electing the tax assessors once every four years."[8] We should not neglect the municipal reformer who blames citizen apathy upon the inherent rascality of politics. He wants to "take government out of politics," and believes that the city manager and his council, having cleansed government, will conquer apathy and secure citizen participation in government.

What is representative government? Jefferson too, it will be recalled, favored it for the government of large territories. But he, like Tom Paine and John Taylor, understood it to mean that when, due to physical handicaps, the people could not assemble together to direct and control government, they employed agents to do so on their behalf and under their instructions. The right of constituents to instruct their representative concerning his official conduct and his duty to obey were clear and beyond dispute. The representative was no more than an ambassador of his sovereign constituents. This view of representative government is clearly incompatible with the concept of political virtue supplied by writers such as Luther Gulick, Roscoe Martin, Robert Wood, and Paul Ylvisaker. Unfortunately, these gentlemen have not addressed themselves to the subject of representative government in any detail. A clue to their position is found in their approving references to Madison's assertion that government should "refine and enlarge the public views," and in their advice that elected representatives should give the people the benefit of their "best judgment." Implicit in their view of the primacy of the community and in their emphasis upon discussion and debate as the means of attaining justice is again a Madisonian and Burkean, rather than a Jeffersonian, view of representation. Madison, it will be recalled, maintained that a "republic," as opposed to a "democracy," would "refine and enlarge the public views by passing them through the medium of a chosen body of citizens, whose wisdom may best discern the *true interest of their country* and whose patriotism and love of justice will be least likely to sacrifice it to *temporary or partial considerations*."[9] (Italics supplied)

A classic statement on representative government, on the relation between electors and their rulers, will be found in two speeches which Edmund Burke addressed to his constituents in Bristol. On November 3, 1774, Cruger and Burke rose to thank the voters of Bristol for electing them to Parliament. Cruger, the senior Member, professed himself to be "the servant of my constituents, not their master, subservient to their will, not superior to it." He promised to carry out faithfully their instructions and mandates. Following Cruger on the hustings, Burke spoke thus:

> Certainly, Gentlemen, it ought to be the happiness and glory of a representative to live in . . . the most unreserved communication with his constituents. Their wishes ought to have great weight with him. . . . But his unbiased opinion, his mature

judgment, his enlightened conscience, he ought not to sacrifice to you, to any man, or to any set of men living. These he does not derive from your pleasure; no, nor from the law and the constitution. These are a trust from Providence, for the abuse of which he is deeply answerable. Your representative owes you . . . his judgment; and he betrays, instead of serving you, if he sacrifices it to your opinion.

My worthy colleague says his will ought to be subservient to yours. . . . But government and legislation are matters of reason and judgment, and not of inclination; and what sort of reason is that, in which the determination precedes the discussion; in which one set of men deliberate, and another decide?[10]

Six years later Burke returned to Bristol to seek reelection. Addressing an alienated electorate in the local Guild Hall, he defended his conduct as a member of Parliament in these historic words:

I did not obey your instructions: No. I conformed to the instructions of truth and nature, and maintained your interest, against your opinions, with a constancy that became me. . . . I am to look, indeed, to your opinions; but to such opinions as you and I must have five years hence. I was not to look to the flash of the day. I knew that you chose me, in my place, along with others, to be a pillar of the state, and not a weathercock on the top of the edifice . . . and of no use but to indicate the shiftings of every fashionable gale.[11]

It may be a sad commentary upon the doctrine of the sovereignty of the individual that the people of Bristol did not reelect Edmund Burke.

Algernon Sidney, William Blackstone, William Paley, John Stuart Mill, and Jeremy Bentham* are some of the other well-known English writers who emphasized the representative's duty to follow his conscience and best judgment; they saw the nation, rather than the electoral district, as the appropriate subject of his care and the locus of his responsibility.

A number of American writers, who place sovereignty with the organic community or nation and favor aristocratic government, endorse the Burkean-Madisonian concept of representative government. Madison's own collaborator on *The Federalist,* Alexander Hamilton, believed that "mechanics" and manufacturers did not, in the normal course of their experience, acquire the abilities essential to the work of a deliberative body. He hoped that the voters would, therefore, not exert more than a "proper degree of influence" upon their representatives. John Adams thought that the people would be well advised to entrust their legislative power to "a few of the most wise and good."

In 1841 Harper and Brothers published a book entitled *Democracy,* characterizing it as the first treatise ever published "the express design of which is to elucidate the democratic theory." The author, George Sidney Camp, wrote to counteract the influence of Blackstone, Paley, and Burke—"the favourers of arbitrary power"—on young minds in the colleges of republican America. He devoted a chapter in his book to a criticism of the "so-called" right of constituents to instruct their representatives. In spite of his declared

---

*Bentham, true to his utilitarian logic, suggests a compromise. If a deputy, after speaking in support of an arrangement, which his constituents do not like, votes against it, he is not acting inconsistently. "By his *speech,* his duty to the public is fulfilled, by his *vote,* his duty to his constituents." Quoted in John A. Fairlie, "The Nature of Political Representation," *American Political Science Review* (April 1940), p. 242.

lack of warmth towards Burke, his theory of representation followed closely the Burkean model.

Claims for a right of instruction are pretentious, wrote Camp. The phrase "the people" must mean the "whole people." The whole people, this "paramount democratic sovereignty," acted directly only to settle the constitution. That accomplished, there was no further occasion for the people to act in their "original, absolute, and sovereign capacity." The town and ward meetings and other "primary" assemblies were organs of public opinion to which wise politicians should pay attention. But they were not organs of the sovereign will which representatives must obey. After electing their representatives, the electors would have no function to perform until the next election. The people had never intended to govern by "imparting to their representatives the momentary changes and impulses of public opinion."[12] Members of Congress were bound to represent the nation at large, not merely their respective electoral districts.

The right of instruction is deemed by its proponents to vest in the majority. Now the right of the majority to rule, argued Camp, is not an absolute moral law but a practical necessity. The minority has a right to influence the majority view, to impress upon it "a just and proper bias." Minorities are persuaded to become loyal members of the civil society on the understanding that the end of all legislation is justice and that decisions in government will be made after due deliberation, exercising that wisdom and rectitude of which men may be capable. Majority decisions would then represent the "settled wisdom of the nation rather than . . . the hasty effervescence of popular passions."[13] Society harbors many different and conflicting interests and viewpoints. These can be harmonized only if the government, pursuing justice, addresses itself to the common interest of all—"the only neutral ground on which all parties can meet" and act together in maintaining a republican community. Hence it is that republican government "separates the legislator from the impulses of passion and the solicitations of private interest, and calls on him to pronounce a just general rule."[14]

Camp's view of representative government is consistent with his general political theory. He concedes that it is a part of man's nature to be free, but this freedom must be exercised according to the moral principles which also are an "essential part of his nature." He cannot have right to do wrong. With Montesquieu, Camp defines liberty as "the power of doing what we ought to will, and the not being constrained to do what we ought not to will." He agrees with Cicero (and Burke, whom he does not mention in this connection) that a republic is "the union of a multitude cemented by an agreement in what is right, and a participation in what is useful."[15] Self-government then is a government of free and deliberative opinion. When the public mind is influenced by passion or fear or unthinking acquiescence, it forms prejudice, not opinion.

Francis Lieber devoted three long chapters in his *Manual of Political Ethics* (apparently one of the first American text books on political science) to a consideration of representative government. His views are remarkably similar to Camp's. He conceded that a legislator should take into account the "sense and sentiment" of his constituents, but he must not act as their "instructed deputy," promoting their limited selfish interests. Once elected he must represent the entire nation, regarding his constituents "as part and parcel of the state, as a living limb of the whole body politic."[16]

The "deputative system" implies, wrote Lieber, that a representative needs to represent only the majority of voters in his district on any given issue before the legislature. But the correct position is that he must represent also the minorities and those who cannot vote or do not have the right to vote. Minorities and the non-voting parts of the populace are equally members of the society. A concept of "virtual representation" is included in the true definition of his function.

Lieber maintains that a representative must, first and foremost, pursue truth and justice disinterestedly in discovering the public interest. These are not necessarily conveyed by the prevailing public opinion. He should follow "true" public opinion, not the momentary "impulse" or "fanaticism" of the masses. At this point, Lieber quotes approvingly from Burke's second speech at Bristol, including the statement: "I am to look indeed to your opinions; but to such opinions as you and I must have five years hence."[17] Only a representative system, he says, can arrive at the political truth. It alone admits of discussion, debate, and deliberation essential to the pursuit of truth and justice.

> Debate, well guided, is an indispensable palladium of civil liberty. Instruction would make, and unfortunately has made, out of deliberative assemblies, assemblies without freedom of deliberation and without freedom of thought, which is a tyranny with painful consequences. Indeed, directing men to vote one way or the other, in a case in which it is nevertheless maintained that previous inquiry ought to guide, is repugnant to all respect for truth and for conscience. . . .

> The true and difficult object in politics . . . is to secure by wise, that is by safe and appropriate, means, the discovery of truth and the empire of mind over matter, chance, force, and bulk.[18]

Lieber characterizes the system of representative government as the "flower" of Western civilization, the result of its passage from feudalism to the modern age. It is "far nobler than a mere approach to some-thing we cannot obtain, the government of the people in the forum, or the ecclesia, to use the Athenian term."[19]

According to Elisha Mulford, who also rejects the deputative system of representation, the function of a representative is to express the "moral personality" of the nation. In his decisions and actions he must uphold the nation's majesty, unity and freedom. He cannot become merely the exponent or agent of an "external will" such as a party or a constituency.[20] Mulford rejects the formula of government by public opinion, because frequently public opinion reflects "unformed thought," taking its "color from the changing impulse and emotion and passion of the moment." It may on occasion indicate the enduring purposes of society, but more often it denotes the "rude and crude" agitation rather than the deliberate thought of the people. The statesman cannot ignore public opinion, but he must know also that public opinion has to be clarified and refined. Instead of guiding the ship of state, it "needs a firmer intelligence to guide it."[21]

John W. Burgess, another nationalist writer who favored aristocratic government,* notes that direct democracy is even less sympathetic to liberty than the direct and personal rule of a monarch.[22] He too rejects the doctrine of instruction. Representation in both houses of Congress is "uninstructed"; the principle being that "each senator and each representative represents the whole United States, according to his own intelligence and judgment, and that there is no con-

---

* "A democratic state," writes Burgess, "may have an aristo-cratic government; and I do not see why, in any condition of society except the perfect, or nearly perfect, this is not the best political system for all states which have attained the demo-cratic form." *Political Science and Comparative Constitutional Law*, II, 4.

stituency in the United States which can demand a
control over its representative in either house of the
Congress, or require his resignation."[23]

Several contemporary American writers have argued
in the same vein. Walter Lippmann, still another advocate of aristocratic government, has been urging the
Burkean concept of representation (and condemning
the Jeffersonian "heresies" concerning direct democracy
and instruction of representatives) for several decades.
In the "traditions of civility," says Lippmann, "while
the electors choose the ruler, they do not own any
shares in him and they have no right to command him.
His duty is to the office and not to his electors. Their
duty is to fill the office and not to direct the office-
holder."[24] The values of truth, justice, and disinterestedness; the instrumental values of discussion and debate;
and a strong distrust of public opinion as a guide to
public policy are among the more important features
of Lippmann's political philosophy. In remarkably similar terms, Senator Fulbright has recently written an
exposition of representative government, which, coming from a legislator, is especially noteworthy. The
Senator maintains that while the people may settle the
grand ends of civil society, and even supply its basic
moral decisions and value judgments, they must not try
to take over the navigation of the ship of state.

A political leader is chosen because of his sup-
posed qualifications for his job. If he is qualified,
he should be allowed to carry it out according to
his own best judgment. If his judgment is found
defective by his electors, he can and should be
removed. His constituents, however, must recognize that he has a duty to his office as well as to
them and that their duty in turn is to fill the office
but not to run it. We must distinguish between the
functions of *representation* and of *government, re-*

quiring our elected leaders to represent us while *allowing* them to govern.[25] (Italics in original)

The subject of representative government deserves greater attention from students of local government, especially metropolitan reformers. For it is impossible to justify metropolitan integration in terms of political values except on the ground that the Madisonian concept of representative government is more desirable, not merely more feasible, than Jefferson's pure republicanism. A further word may be said concerning the relevance of the theories explored above to the organizational problem of American local government. Emphasizing the sovereignty of the individual, we are likely to endorse the Jeffersonian preference for direct democracy. We are likely to support smaller units of government: small town against the big city, city against the state, the state against the federal government. We will then oppose the integration of localities into larger governmental units to solve metropolitan area problems. For such problems we will seek non-political, even nongovernmental, solutions. If, following the "laws of power," we invest the state or the nation with absolute and indivisible sovereignty, we lay the groundwork for despotism. On the other hand, if we recognize the corporate community (or the corporate nation) and concede that the community as well as the individual has rights, we arrive at the concept of a "half-sovereign" individual living under limited government. Admitting that the rights of the individual must be accommodated to the claims of the community, and vice versa, we get the theoretical framework for a representative and constitutional democracy. The smallness of jurisdictions is then no longer necessary for obtaining democratic virtue. Philosophical objections to new arrangements in governmental organization disappear.

Natural rights, the social contract, sovereignty of the

individual, direct democracy, individualism, laissez faire, weak government, are American values. But it should be emphasized that supremacy of the organic community, the sovereignty of reason, discussion and debate, disinterestedness in the pursuit of truth and justice, liberty for all including the dissident, representative democracy, vigor of government in the service of the people, are equally American values. In its origins neither set of values is any more "foreign" than the other.

Notes and References

CHAPTER 1: INTRODUCTION

1. Robert C. Wood, "A Division of Powers in Metropolitan Areas," in Arthur Maass, ed., *Area and Power* (Glencoe: The Free Press, 1959), pp. 58–60.
2. Jacques Maritain, "The Concept of Sovereignty," *American Political Science Review* (June 1950), 343ff.
3. *The Federalist,* No. 9.
4. *Ibid.,* No. 32.
5. Quoted in Charles E. Merriam, *History of the Theory of Sovereignty Since Rousseau* (New York: Columbia University Press, 1900), p. 163.
6. *The Federalist,* Nos. 39, 40, 62.
7. Gillard Hunt, ed. *The Writings of James Madison* (New York: G. P. Putnam's Sons, 1910), IX, 572.
8. *The Federalist,* No. 9.
9. Frederick Grimke, *Nature and Tendency of Free Institutions* (Cincinnati: 1848), pp. 519–520, 527; Nathaniel Chipman, *Principles of Government* (Burlington: 1833, First edition 1793), pp. 142ff, 273; E. D. Mansfield, *The Political Grammar of the United States* (New York: 1834), pp. 520–521; John Taylor, *New Views of the Constitution* (Washington: 1823), sec. 13. Brief but appropriate quotations from these works will be found in Merriam's *History of the Theory*

of Sovereignty, pp. 164–166 and also his *A History of American Political Theories* (New York: Macmillan, 1903), pp. 260ff.

10. See, for instance, *Chisholm* v. *Georgia*, 2 Dall. 419 (1793); *Ware* v. *Hylton*, 3 Dall. 232 (1796); *Cherokee Nation* v. *Georgia*, 5 Peters 26 (1831); *McCulloch* v. *Maryland*, 4 Wheat. 316 (1819); *Worcester* v. *Georgia*, 6 Pet. 591–592 (1832); *Tenn.* v. *Davis*, 10 Otto 226 (1879).

11. *The Federalist*, No. 46.

12. *History of the Theory of Sovereignty*, p. 167.

13. Speech on the "Force Bill" in the United States Senate, February 15 and 16, 1833, in Richard K. Cralle, ed., *The Works of John C. Calhoun* (New York: D. Appleton and Co., 1854), II, 232.

14. Francis Lieber, *A Manual of Political Ethics* (Philadelphia: J. B. Lippincott, 1881, first published 1838), I, 216.

15. John W. Burgess, *Political Science and Comparative Constitutional Law* (Boston: Ginn and Co., 1896), I, 52.

16. Lieber, *op. cit.*, p. 219.

17. Francis Lieber, "Nationalism and Internationalism," *Miscellaneous Writings* (Philadelphia: J. B. Lippincott, 1881), II, 228. Lieber dismissed the "state of nature" as having no basis in fact. He did not altogether reject the contract and natural law and rights theories. But he was careful to point out that he did not interpret these theories as the seventeenth and eighteenth century revolutionists had understood them. Other writers—Brownson, Jameson, Mulford, Burgess, Woodrow Wilson, Willoughby—discarded these theories with even less reservation. Natural rights had no place in politics, for there were no rights or liberties "outside of state organization." They had at best only an "ethical value." Willoughby denied that they had even this. See Merriam, *A History of American Political Theories*, pp. 306–311.

18. John A. Jameson, *The Constitutional Convention* (New York: Charles Scribner, 1867), pp. 19–20, 28ff.

19. Elisha Mulford, *The Nation* (Boston: Houghton, Mifflin, 1888), p. 129 and *passim*.

20. Burgess, *Political Science and Comparative Constitutional Law*, I, 55, 79ff.

21. *Ibid.*, I, 80.

22. John W. Burgess, "The American Commonwealth: Changes in Its Relation to the Nation," *Political Science Quarterly* (March 1886), p. 23.

23. *Ibid.*, p. 32.

24. *Ibid.*, p. 34.

25. Burgess, *Political Science and Comparative Constitutional Law*, I, 44ff.

26. *Ibid.*, I, 85.

27. Lieber, *A Manual of Political Ethics,* I, 173. A similar view is expressed by Theodore Woolsey (who, incidentally, edited the second edition of Lieber's *Political Ethics*). He maintains that the function of the State includes, among other things, cultivation of the spiritual nature of man by educating his religious nature, moral sense, taste, and intellect. See Woolsey's *Political Science* (New York: Scribner, Armstrong, 1878), I, Chap. 4, Sections 75–80.

28. John Dewey, *Individualism Old and New* (New York: Capricorn Books, 1962, first published 1929), p. 72.

29. See especially Walter Lippmann's *Public Opinion* (New York: Macmillan, 1922); *The Phantom Public* (New York: Harcourt, Brace, 1925); *The Public Philosophy* (Boston: Little, Brown, 1955).

30. *City Politics* (Cambridge: Harvard University Press and M.I.T. Press, 1963), p. 139.

31. *Ibid.*, p. 154.

32. *Ibid.*, pp. 170–171.

33. Albert B. Hart, "Growth of American Theories of Popular Government," *American Political Science Review* (August 1907), 557–558.

34. Merriam, *A History of American Political Theories,* pp. 332–333.

CHAPTER 2: THE POPULAR THEORY

1. For the text of the early Rhode Island compacts, see Amasa M. Eaton, "The Right to Local Self-Government," *Harvard Law Review,* I (February 1900), 449.

2. *Ibid.*

3. Amasa M. Eaton, "The Right to Local Self-Government," *Harvard Law Review,* II (March 1900), 575.

4. Amasa M. Eaton, "The Right to Local Self-Government," *Harvard Law Review,* V (June 1900), 137.

5. *Ibid.*

6. *Ibid.*, p. 138.

7. *Ibid.*, pp. 119–121.

8. Frank J. Goodnow, *Municipal Home Rule* (New York: Macmillan, 1897), p. 20. Also see Howard Lee McBain, *The Law and Practice of Municipal Home Rule* (New York: Columbia University Press, 1916), p. 5.

9. This is the opening statement of Chapter IV, entitled "The Principle of the Sovereignty of the People of America," in *Democracy in America,* The Henry Reeve Text, Phillips Bradley, ed. (New York: Alfred A. Knopf, 1953), I.

10. *Ibid.*, pp. 56–57.
11. *Ibid.*, pp. 64–65.
12. *Ibid.*, p. 65.
13. *Ibid.*, p. 65.
14. *Ibid.*, p. 67.
15. *Ibid.*, p. 61.
16. *Ibid.*, p. 89.
17. *Ibid.*, p. 90.
18. *Ibid.*
19. *Ibid.*, p. 92.
20. *Ibid.*, p. 95.
21. *Ibid.*, p. 60.
22. Robert C. Wood, *Suburbia* (New York: Houghton, Mifflin, 1958), p. 108.
23. Tocqueville, *op. cit.*, p. 60.
24. *Ibid.*
25. *Ibid.*, p. 259.
26. *Ibid.*, p. 262.
27. *Ibid.*, p. 263.
28. *Ibid.*, p. 264.
29. *Ibid.*, p. 3.
30. Alexis de Tocqueville, *Democracy in America,* The Henry Reeve Text, Phillips Bradley, ed. (New York: Alfred A. Knopf, 1953), II, 197, 318, 99.
31. *Ibid.*, p. 98.
32. *Ibid.*, p. 97.
33. *Ibid.*, pp. 293–294.
34. *Ibid.*, p. 142.
35. *Ibid.*, pp. 136–137.
36. *Ibid.*, p. 142.
37. *Ibid.*, p. 290.
38. *Ibid.*, p. 318.
39. *Ibid.*, p. 319.
40. Tocqueville, *Democracy in America,* I, 46.
41. Letter to John Adams on October 28, 1813, in Paul L. Ford, ed., *The Works of Thomas Jefferson* (New York: G. P. Putnam's Sons, 1905), XI, 347. All subsequent references to Jefferson's *Works* relate to the same edition unless otherwise stated.
42. *Works,* XI, 347.
43. *Works,* XII, 9.
44. *Ibid.*
45. *Works,* IX, 18.
46. *Ibid.*, p. 140 (Letter to Gideon Granger dated August 13, 1800).
47. *Works,* IX, 17.
48. *Ibid.*, p. 197.

49. *Works,* XI, 529.

50. *Ibid.,* p. 528.

51. *Works,* XI, 534.

52. *Ibid.*

53. *Works,* XII, 12. A similar statement will be found in Jefferson's letter to Taylor dated May 28, 1816. He wrote: "Every generation coming equally, by the laws of the Creator of the world, to the free possession of the earth He made for their subsistence, unincumbered by their predecessors, who, like them, were but tenants for life." *Works,* XI, 529.

54. For a good discussion of Jefferson's anti-urban, anti-industrial biases, see Morton and Lucia White, *The Intellectual Versus the City* (Cambridge: Harvard University Press, 1962), pp. 12–20.

55. Locke's influence in America is acknowledged at all hands. It may be of interest to note that he was one of Jefferson's three greatest men ever; the other two being Newton and Bacon.

56. John Locke, *An Essay Concerning the True Original, Extent and End of Civil Government* (1690), Second Essay, sect. 7.

57. *Ibid.,* sect. 87.

58. *Ibid.,* sect. 149.

59. *Ibid.,* sect. 89, 95.

60. *Ibid.,* sect. 113.

61. *Ibid.,* sect. 121.

62. *Ibid.,* sect. 129, 130.

63. *Ibid.,* sect. 13.

64. *Ibid.,* sect. 124.

65. For an elaboration of this point, see Raymond Polin, "Justice in Locke's Philosophy," in *Nomos* (Justice) (1963), VI, 266ff.

66. Locke, *op. cit.,* sect. 134.

67. Roscoe C. Martin, *Grass Roots* (University, Alabama: University of Alabama Press, 1957), p. 5.

68. *Ibid.,* p. 4.

69. *Ibid.,* pp. 4–5.

70. *Ibid.,* p. 32.

71. Wood, *Suburbia,* p. 18.

72. *Ibid.,* p. 85.

73. *Ibid.,* p. 87.

CHAPTER 3: SOVEREIGN OR VASSAL?

1. In his *Commentaries on the Law of Municipal Corporations* (5th ed., Vol. I, sec. 98), Dillon wrote: "It must now be conceded that the great weight of authority denies *in toto* the

existence, in the absence of special constitutional provisions, of *any inherent right of local self-government which is beyond legislative control."* (Italics in original) Quoted approvingly in Howard Lee McBain, *The Law and the Practice of Municipal Home Rule* (New York: Columbia University Press, 1916), p. 15.

2. Eaton, "The Right to Local Self-Government," I, *Harvard Law Review* (February 1900), 447.

3. Eugene McQuillin, *The Law of Municipal Corporations* (New York: Callaghan and Co., 1928), I, 255.

4. Eaton, *op. cit.,* p. 442.

5. Amasa M. Eaton, "The Origin of Municipal Incorporation in England and in the United States," *Report of the American Bar Association* (Philadelphia, 1902), p. 294.

6. A listing of the cases where judges reiterated or supported the Cooley doctrine follows: *People* v. *Draper,* 15 N. Y. (1857), (See Judge Brown's dissent); *People* v. *Lothrop,* 24 Mich. 235 (1872); *People* v. *Albertson,* 55 N. Y. 50 (1873); *People* v. *The Common Council of Detroit,* 28 Mich. 228 (1873); *Park Commissioners* v. *The Mayor & C.,* 29 Mich. 343 (1874); *People* v. *Lynch,* 51 Cal. 15 (1875); *Allor* v. *Wayne County Auditors,* 43 Mich. 76 (1880); *The People* v. *Porter,* 90 N. Y. 68 (1882); *People* v. *Harding,* 53 Mich. 481 (1884); *Robertson* v. *Baxter,* 57 Mich. 127 (1885); *Attorney General* v. *Detroit,* 58 Mich. 213 (1885); *Wilcox* v. *Paddock,* 65 Mich. 23 (1887); *Holt* v. *Denny,* 118 Ind. 382 (1888); *City of Evansville* v. *State,* 118 Ind. 426 (1888); *Board of Metropolitan Police* v. *the Board of Auditors,* 68 Mich. 676 (1888); *Rathbone* v. *Wirth,* 150 N. Y. 459 (1896); *Helena Consolidated Water Co.* v. *Steele,* 20 Mont. 1 (1897); *State* v. *Moores,* 76 N. Rep. 175 (1898); *State ex. rel. Attorney General* v. *Kennedy,* 60 Neb. 300 (1900); *Moreland* v. *Millen,* 126 Mich. 228 (1901); *State ex. rel. Genke* v. *Fox,* 128 Ind. 126 (1902); *City of Lexington* v. *Thompson,* 113 Ky. 540 (1902); *State ex rel. White* v. *Barker,* 116 Iowa 96 (1902); *Ex Parte Lewis,* 45 Tex. Cr. 1 (1903); *Davidson* v. *Hine,* 151 Mich. 294 (1908); *State* v. *Lynch,* 88 Ohio 71 (1913). See Judge Wanamaker's dissent; *Kalamazoo* v. *Titus,* 208 Mich. 252 (1919); *Attorney General* v. *Detroit,* 225 Mich. 631 (1923). This listing is not comprehensive. Note also that, as one might expect, judges in these cases have endorsed the views of Judge Cooley in varying measure.

7. *People* v. *Draper,* 15 N. Y. (1857), p. 561. The case concerned the constitutional validity of a New York State law that authorized the state legislature to abolish the police organizations of New York City and Brooklyn, replacing them with a metropolitan police district whose commissioners were to be

appointed by the state. The State Supreme Court sustained the law. For further details see *Infra.*

8. *Ibid.,* p. 561.

9. *Ibid.,* p. 574.

10. *People* v. *Hurlbut,* 24 Mich. (1871), pp. 87–88.

11. *Ibid.,* p. 89.

12. *Ibid.,* p. 96.

13. *Ibid.,* p. 107.

14. *Ibid.,* p. 99.

15. *Ibid.,* p. 101.

16. *Ibid.,* p. 108.

17. Thomas McIntyre Cooley, *Constitutional Limitations* (Boston: Little, Brown, 1890, first published 1868), p. 225.

18. *Ibid.,* p. 281. Also see Cooley's *The General Principles of Constitutional Law* (Boston: Little, Brown, 1898, first published 1880), p. 378.

19. Cooley, *The General Principles of Constitutional Law,* p. 379. Also see *Constitutional Limitations,* pp. 227ff.

20. Cooley, *The General Principles of Constitutional Law,* p. 39.

21. Thomas McIntyre Cooley, "The Federal Supreme Court —Its Place in the American Constitutional System," in Cooley and others, *Constitutional History of the United States* (New York: G. P. Putnam's Sons, 1889), p. 32. See also Cooley, *The General Principles of Constitutional Law,* p. 23.

22. Cooley, *Constitutional Limitations,* p. 704.

23. Benjamin R. Twiss, *Lawyers and the Constitution: How Laissez Faire Came to the Supreme Court* (Princeton: Princeton University Press, 1942), p. 18.

24. Edward S. Corwin, *Liberty Against Government* (Baton Rouge: Louisiana State University Press, 1948), p. 116. For accounts of Cooley's eminence and influence see Twiss, *op. cit.,* pp. 18–41; Clyde E. Jacobs, *Law Writers and the Courts* (Berkeley: University of California Press, 1954), *passim.* For many years Cooley was a professor of law and dean of the University of Michigan law school. Among his students who subsequently rose to eminence was Mr. Justice Sutherland.

25. Some of the cases decided along the Dillon Rule are: *People* v. *Draper,* 15 N. Y. 532 (1857); *Mayor & C.* v. *State & C.,* 15 Md. 376 (1859); *State* v. *County Court & C.,* 34 Mo. 546 (1864); *Booth* v. *Town of Woodbury,* 32 Conn. 118 (1864); *Webster* v. *Town of Harwinton,* 32 Conn. 131 (1864); *People* v. *Mahaney,* 13 Mich. 481 (1865); *People* v. *Shepard,* 36 N. Y. 285 (1867); *City of Clinton* v. *Cedar Rapids and Missouri Railroad Co.,* 24 Iowa 455 (1868); *Philadelphia* v. *Fox,* 64 Penna. St. 169 (1870); *Town of Duanesburgh* v. *Jenkins,* 57 N. Y. 177 (1874); *Barnes* v. *District of Columbia,*

91 U.S. 540 (1875); *State* v. *Covington*, 29 Ohio St. 102 (1876); *Pumphrey* v. *Mayor & C.*, 47 Md. 145 (1877); *Burch* v. *Hardwicke*, 30 Gratt. 24 (1878); *Perkins* v. *Slack*, 86 Penna. St. 270 (1878); *Mt. Pleasant* v. *Beckwith*, 100 U.S. 514 (1879); *Mereweather* v. *Garret*, 102 U.S. 472 (1880); *Ewing* v. *Hoblitzelle*, 85 Mo. 77 (1884); *Coyle* v. *McIntire*, 7 Houston (Del.) 44 (1884); *Darby* v. *Sharon Hill*, 112 Penna. St. 70 (1886); *State* v. *Smith*, 44 Ohio St. 348 (1886); *State* v. *Hunter*, 38 Kans. 578 (1888); *Met. R. Co.* v. *Dist. of Columbia*, 132 U.S. 1 (1889); *Commonwealth* v. *Plaisted*, 148 Mass. 386 (1889); *Grimble* v. *People*, 19 Col. 187 (1893); *State* v. *Williams*, 68 Conn. 131 (1896); *State ex rel. Clausen* v. *Burr*, 65 Wash. 524 (1911); *State ex rel.* v. *Thompson*, 149 Wis. 488 (1912); *Harris* v. *Wm. R. Compton Bond Co.*, 244 Mo. 664 (1912); *Bayville* v. *Boothbay Harbor*, 110 Me. 46 (1912); *Booten* v. *Pinson*, 77 W. Va. 412 (1915); *Rylands* v. *Clark*, 278 Ill. 39 (1917); *City of Reno* v. *Stoddard*, 40 Nev. 537 (1917); *Smiddy* v. *Ternton* v. *New Jersey*, 262 U.S. 182 (1923). For a fuller statewide listing consult McQuillin, *op. cit.*, sec. 186. McQuillin does not indicate the year each case was decided. But in this omission he is not alone.

26. *People* v. *Draper*, 15 N. Y. (1857), p. 543.

27. *Ibid.*, p. 549.

28. Quoted in *City of Clinton* v. *The Cedar Rapids and Missouri River Railroad Co.*, 24 Iowa 455 (1868), pp. 462, 463.

29. *Ibid.*, p. 475.

30. Judge Dillon expressed this view in his subsequent writings also. In his *Commentaries on the Law of Municipal Corporations* (4th ed., p. 145), he observed: "It is a general and undisputed proposition of law that a municipal corporation possesses and can exercise the following powers and no others: First, those granted in express words; second, those necessarily or fairly implied in or incident to the powers expressly granted; third, those essential to the declared objects and purposes of the corporation—not simply convenient but indispensable. Any fair reasonable doubt concerning the existence of power is resolved by the courts against the corporation and the power is denied." Quoted, after attributing to Judge Dillon's work unequalled authoritativeness, by Frank J. Goodnow in *City Government in the United States* (New York: The Century Co., 1904), p. 74.

31. Quoted by Judge Eugene McQuillin in *The Law of Municipal Corporations*, I, 507*n*.

32. *City of Trenton* v. *the State of New Jersey*, 262 U.S. 182 (1923). Note the close resemblance between the words of Justice Butler and those of Judge Dillon quoted earlier.

33. From an opinion of Mr. Justice Moody in *Hunter* v. *Pittsburgh,* 207 U.S. 161, quoted approvingly by Justice Butler in the *City of Trenton* v. *the State of New Jersey,* pp. 186–87.

34. Andrew C. McLaughlin, *A Constitutional History of the United States* (New York: Appleton-Century-Crofts, 1935), pp. 457–458.

35. 3 Alabama 137, 143 (1841). For other expressions of the same view, see McLaughlin, *op. cit.,* p. 460.

36. *Charles River Bridge* v. *Warren Bridge,* 11 Peters 457–458 (1837).

37. *State* v. *Thompson,* 149 Wis. (1912), p. 501.

38. *Ibid.,* p. 502.

39. *Ibid.,* pp. 503–504.

40. *Ibid.,* p. 505.

CHAPTER 4: GOVERNMENT BY THE PEOPLE

1. William B. Munro, ed., *The Initiative, Referendum and Recall* (New York: D. Appleton, 1912), p. 6.

2. *Ibid.,* p. 13.

3. George W. Guthrie, "The Initiative, Referendum and Recall," *Annals of the American Academy of Political and Social Science* (hereafter referred to as *Annals*), September 1912; and Robert T. Paine, "The Development of Direct Legislation in America," in Munro, ed., *The Initiative, Referendum and Recall.*

4. Lewis J. Johnson, "Direct Legislation as an Ally of Representative Government," in Munro, *op. cit.,* p. 148.

5. *Ibid.,* p. 149.

6. *Ibid.,* p. 158.

7. Jonathan Bourne, Jr., "A Defense of Direct Legislation," in Munro, *op. cit.,* pp. 196–197.

8. Jonathan Bourne, "Functions of the Initiative, Referendum and Recall," *Annals* (September 1912), p. 9.

9. *Ibid.,* p. 3.

10. John R. Commons, "Referendum and Initiative in City Government," *Political Science Quarterly* (December 1902), p. 625.

11. *Ibid.,* p. 626.

12. Theodore Roosevelt, "Nationalism and Popular Rule," *Outlook* (January 21, 1911), reproduced in Munro, *op. cit.,* pp. 52–68.

13. Woodrow Wilson, "The Issues of Reform," *North American Review* (May 1910), reproduced in Munro, *op. cit.,* pp. 69–79.

14. Samuel W. McCall, "Representative as Against Direct Legislation," *Atlantic* (October 1911), reproduced in Munro, *op. cit.,* p. 165.

15. Charles M. Hollingsworth, "The So-Called Progressive Movement," *Annals* (September 1912), p. 35.

16. *Ibid.,* pp. 36–47.

17. Munro, ed., *The Initiative, Referendum and Recall,* 1912. See his Introduction, pp. 17–26. See also his *The Government of American Cities* (New York: Macmillan, 1913), pp. 343–353.

18. Munro, *The Government of American Cities,* p. 343.

19. *Ibid.,* pp. 346–349.

20. Gamaliel Bradford, *The Lesson of Popular Government.* (New York: Macmillan, 1899), II, 197–201.

21. Henry Jones Ford, "Direct Legislation and the Recall," *Annals* (September 1912), p. 70.

22. Ellis P. Oberholtzer, *The Referendum in America* (New York: Charles Scribner's Son, 1911, first published 1900), p. 392.

23. *Ibid.,* p. 511.

24. *Ibid.,* p. 513.

25. Horace E. Deming, *Government of American Cities* (New York: G. P. Putnam's Son, 1909), pp. 116–117.

26. *Ibid.,* pp. 156–157.

27. *Ibid.,* p. 184.

28. Frederick C. Howe, *The Modern City and Its Problems* (New York: Charles Scribner's Son, 1915), p. 76.

29. *Ibid.,* pp. 60–61.

30. Cited in Howard E. Dean, "J. Allen Smith: Jeffersonian Critic," *American Political Science Review* (December 1956), p. 1102.

31. Barnet Hodes, "Wanted: A New Road to Municipal Home Rule," *National Municipal Review* (December 1941), p. 691.

32. William F. Devin, "The People Can, Must Do It," *National Municipal Review* (December 1949), p. 552.

33. *Ibid.,* p. 551.

34. *Ibid.,* p. 552.

35. Rodney L. Mott, "Strengthening Home Rule," *National Municipal Review* (April 1950), p. 174.

36. *Ibid.,* p. 174.

37. *Ibid.,* p. 177. For another endorsement of local "rights," local claim to autonomy and to equality of status with the state, see: Frank C. Moore, "Toward Firmer Foundation," *National Municipal Review* (January 1949), pp. 17–20, 25. Moore was then Comptroller of New York State and had been previously executive secretary of the New York Association of

Towns. See also a policy resolution on this subject passed by the American Municipal Association at its annual convention at Washington, D.C. in December 1948. This is mentioned in some detail in the *National Municipal Review* (January 1949), and endorsed editorially in its issue of March 1949.

38. Commission on Intergovernmental Relations, *An Advisory Committee Report on Local Government* (Washington, D.C.: U.S. Government Printing Office, June 1955), p. 9. The composition of the committee is significant. Of its ten members, nine were connected with local government in one manner or another. Included were Presidents of the American Municipal Association, National Municipal League, United States Conference of Mayors, and National Association of County Officials.

39. *Ibid.*, p. 29.

40. Delos F. Wilcox, *Municipal Government in Michigan and Ohio, A Study in the Relation of City and Commonwealth* (New York: Columbia University Studies in History, Economics and Public Law, 1896), V, 176.

41. Lieber, *Miscellaneous Writings,* p. 215.

42. Delos F. Wilcox, *The Study of City Government* (New York: Macmillan, 1897), pp. 6, 10.

43. Charles A. Beard, *American City Government* (New York: The Century Company, 1912), pp. 14, 39–40.

44. Frank J. Goodnow, "Municipal Home Rule," *Political Science Quarterly* (March 1906), p. 82.

45. *Ibid.*, pp. 85–86.

46. Frank J. Goodnow, *Municipal Problems* (New York: Columbia University Press, 1911), pp. 20–21.

47. Munro, *The Government of American Cities,* pp. 63–64.

48. *Ibid.*, p. 76.

49. Brian Chapman, *Introduction to French Local Government* (London: Allen and Unwin, 1953), p. 11. On central administrative control see chapter IV and *passim*.

CHAPTER 5: COMMUNITY AND GOVERNMENT

1. Edward C. Banfield and James Q. Wilson, *City Politics* (Cambridge: Harvard University Press and M.I.T. Press, 1963), p. 68.

2. Editorial comment in *National Municipal Review* (December 1935), p. 662.

3. *Ibid.*, p. 689.

4. Wilcox, *The Study of City Government,* pp. 70–71, 93.

5. Goodnow, *Municipal Problems,* pp. 287–307.

6. Munro, *The Government of American Cities,* pp. 66–67.

7. William B. Munro, *Municipal Government and Administration* (New York: Macmillan, 1923), I, 437.

8. Paul Studenski, *The Government of Metropolitan Areas* (New York: National Municipal League, 1930), p. 31.

9. Victor Jones, *Metropolitan Government* (Chicago: University of Chicago Press, 1942), pp. xix–xx.

10. Robert Brooks, "Metropolitan Free Cities," *Political Science Quarterly* (June 1915), p. 222.

11. *Ibid.,* pp. 228–229.

12. *Ibid.,* p. 230.

13. Cited in W. Brooke Graves, "The Future of the American States," *American Political Science Review* (February 1936), pp. 25, 29–30, 41–43.

14. Carl E. McCombs, "Local Self-Government and the State," *National Municipal Review* (April 1937), p. 171.

15. Kirk H. Porter, "County Home Rule A Mistake," *National Municipal Review* (October 1934), p. 519.

16. Theodore B. Manny, "Rural Areas for Rural Government," *National Municipal Review* (August 1932), p. 481.

17. H. G. Wells, *Mankind in the Making* (Leipzig: Bernard Tauchnitz, 1903). The address is reprinted in Williams and Press, *Democracy in Urban America* (Chicago: Rand McNally, 1961). References below relate to this reprint. Wells's views would appear to have had some influence on American thinking. His address to the Fabians is included in several books on American local government and is approvingly referred to in a number of others.

18. Wells, *op. cit.,* pp. 146–147.

19. *Ibid.,* pp. 149–150.

20. *Ibid.,* p. 153.

21. Editorial comment in *National Municipal Review* (February 1948), p. 71.

22. Editorial comment in *National Municipal Review* (November 1958).

23. Joseph H. Crowley, "Home Rule for 'Whole City,'" *National Municipal Review* (April 1950); George H. Deming, "Metro and Little Places," *National Civic Review* (June 1961); Kenneth C. Tollenor, "A Home Rule Puzzle," *National Civic Review* (September 1961).

24. Commission on Intergovernmental Relations, *Report,* 1955, p. 54. See also *Report on State-Local Relations* (prepared for the same Commission), p. 198.

25. Luther Gulick, "Do It Yourself," *National Municipal Review* (December 1957), p. 561.

26. John Stuart Mill, *Representative Government* (New York: Henry Holt, 1875), pp. 183, 452.

27. Willoughby, *An Introduction to the Problems of Government* (New York: 1927), p. 453.

28. Luther Gulick, "New Era, New Thinking," *National Municipal Review* (April 1959), p. 176.

29. Luther Gulick, *The Metropolitan Problem and American Ideas* (New York: Alfred A. Knopf, 1962), p. 55.

30. *Ibid.*, p. 60. *Cf.* Lee in "Home Rule Appraised," *National Civic Review* (October 1962).

31. Gulick, *op. cit.*, p. 61.

32. Robert C. Wood, "A Division of Powers in Metropolitan Areas," in Arthur Maass, ed., *Area and Power* (Glencoe: The Free Press, 1959), pp. 68–69.

33. Gulick, *The Metropolitan Problem and American Ideas,* pp. 125–126.

34. Paul Ylvisaker, "Some Criteria for a 'Proper' Areal Division of Governmental Powers," in *Area and Power,* p. 42. Note that Ylvisaker agrees with Gulick. In the paper referred to here, he notes (p. 37): "And as we sometimes too painfully have experienced, loyalty is as much generated by the very creation and symbolism of boundary lines, as it is by whatever elements of alikeness these lines may happen to include."

35. Quoted without approval in Wood, *Suburbia,* p. 94.

36. *Ibid.*, p. 106.

37. Editorial comment in *National Municipal Review* (February 1948), p. 72.

38. Wood, *Suburbia,* p. 288.

CHAPTER 6: POLITICAL VIRTUE IN THE GOOD COMMUNITY

1. Editorial comment in *National Municipal Review* (April 1959), p. 173. Gulick writes: "If the engineering requirements call for a wider geographic area for real efficiency . . . a way must be found to use the broader jurisdiction for such activities." *The Metropolitan Problem and American Ideas,* p. 140.

2. George H. Deming, "Metro and Little Places," *National Municipal Review* (June 1961), p. 305.

3. Gulick,, *op. cit.*, p. 122.

4. "Call to Action," *National Municipal Review* (January 1942), p. 9.

5. Richard S. Childs, *Civic Victories, The Story of an Unfinished Revolution* (New York: Harper, 1952), p. 3.

6. Editorial comment in *National Municipal Review* (December 1958), p. 545. Also see editorial comment July 1950.

7. Editorial comment in *National Municipal Review* (September 1948), p. 410.

8. Editorial comment in *National Municipal Review* (October 1942), p. 474.

9. Editorial comment in *National Municipal Review* (July 1948), p. 356.

10. *The Federalist,* No. 10.

11. Samuel P. Huntington, "The Founding Fathers and the Division of Powers," in *Area and Power,* pp. 189–190.

12. Paul Ylvisaker, "Some Criteria for a 'Proper' Areal Division of Powers," in *Area and Power,* p. 37.

13. *Ibid.,* pp. 37–38.

14. *Ibid.,* p. 42.

15. Martin, *Grass Roots,* Chapters II and III.

16. *Ibid.,* p. 87.

17. *Ibid.,* p. 81.

18. *Ibid.,* pp. 81–82.

19. Wood, "A Division of Powers in Metropolitan Areas," in *Area and Power,* p. 65.

20. Wood, *Suburbia,* p. 275.

21. *Ibid.,* p. 278.

22. *Ibid.,* p. 281.

23. *Ibid.,* p. 282.

24. *Ibid.,* p. 284.

25. *Ibid.,* p. 293.

26. *Ibid.,* p. 295.

27. *Ibid.,* pp. 297–298.

28. Aristotle, *Politics,* Ernest P. Barker, trans. (London: Oxford University Press, 1950), p. 7.

29. *Ibid.,* p. 391.

30. *Ibid.,* pp. 137–138.

31. *Ibid.,* pp. 108–109.

32. *Ibid.,* pp. 275, 302.

33. *Ibid.,* pp. 148, 172.

34. *Ibid.,* p. 141.

CHAPTER 7: THE WEB OF GOVERNMENT

1. Woodrow Wilson, "Issues of Reform," in Munro, ed., *The Initiative, Referendum and Recall,* p. 79.

2. Quoted in an editorial note in the *National Civic Review* (June 1961), p. 292. Also quoted in the same *Review,* February 1954.

3. See W. Brooke Graves, "The Future of American States," *American Political Science Review* (February 1936), pp. 24ff.

4. W. B. Munro, "Do We Need Regional Governments?" *Forum* (January 1928), p. 109.

5. Senator Joseph S. Clark, "Toward National Federalism," in *The Federal Government and the Cities* (Washington, D.C., 1961), p. 47.

6. Christian A. Herter, "New Horizons for States," *National Municipal Review* (April 1957), p. 176. In supplying a philosophy of federal-state relations, Governor Herter suggested a working principle for demarcating the spheres of federal and state concern: the federal government should confine its assistance, and the direction that goes with it, "to those things that are physical, leaving to the states the administration of those things that deal with individual human beings." *Ibid.*

7. Mark O. Hatfield, "The Role of the States," *National Municipal Review* (December 1959), p. 563.

8. Mitchell Sviridoff, "Headaches Ahead," *National Municipal Review* (February 1960), p. 66.

9. July 1954, p. 328.

10. Roscoe Martin, "Washington and the Cities," in *The Federal Government and the Cities*, p. 3.

11. Andrew Hacker, "Message on the State of the States," *New York Times* Magazine (July 22, 1962), p. 21.

12. R. L. Carleton, *Local Government and Administration in Louisiana* (Baton Rouge: 1935), pp. 301–02.

13. Virgil Sheppard, "The Middle Way–American Plan," *National Municipal Review* (May 1940), p. 297.

14. Wilson W. Wyatt, "The Self-Reliant City," *National Municipal Review* (January 1948), p. 4.

15. Luther Gulick, "Do It Yourself," *National Municipal Review* (December 1957), p. 562.

16. Eugene C. Lee, "Home Rule Appraised," *National Civic Review* (October 1962), p. 488.

17. Thomas H. Reed, "Hope for Suburbanitis," *National Civic Review* (December 1950), p. 543.

18. Thomas H. Reed, "A Call for Plain Talk," *National Civic Review* (March 1962), p. 12.

19. Edward S. Corwin, *Constitutional Revolution, Ltd.* (Claremont: Claremont Colleges, 1941), p. 99.

20. John M. Gaus, *Reflections on Public Administration* (University, Alabama: University of Alabama Press, 1947), p. 80.

21. William Anderson, *The Nation and the States, Rivals or Partners* (Minneapolis: University of Minnesota Press, 1955), p. 145.

22. Paul Ylvisaker, "Some Criteria for a Proper Areal Division of Governmental Powers," in *Area and Power*, p. 35.

23. *Ibid.*, p. 40.

24. *Ibid.*, p. 44.

25. Gulick, *The Metropolitan Problem and American Ideas,* pp. 44, 129–130.

26. *Ibid.,* p. 117.

27. *Ibid.,* pp. 128–129.

28. *Ibid.,* p. 31.

29. *Ibid.,* pp. 134–135.

30. Commission on Intergovernmental Relations, *Report* (1955), p. 5.

31. *Ibid.,* p. 59.

32. *Ibid.,* p. 2.

33. Editorial comment in *National Municipal Review* (July 1954), p. 447.

34. Cecil H. Underwood, "Usurpation a Myth," *National Municipal Review* (November 1958), p. 508.

35. W. Brooke Graves, "Maze of Governments," *National Municipal Review* (May 1960), p. 231. For other expressions of the same general view see also: Joseph E. McLean, "Threat to Responsible Rule," *National Municipal Review* (September 1951); Robert E. Merriam, "Partners or Rivals," *National Municipal Review* (December 1956). Merriam's piece is especially worthy of note because at the time of writing it he was an assistant director in the U. S. Bureau of the Budget under President Eisenhower and professed, in the same article, to subscribe to the President's view that the states had created the federal government and that the creature should not supersede the creator.

36. Robert F. Wagner, "Help for Our Cities," *National Municipal Review* (January 1960), p. 8. Also see Ben West, "Federal-City Relations from the Cities' Point of View," in *The Federal Government and the Cities,* pp. 17–27.

37. Joseph S. Clark, "Toward National Federalism," in *The Federal Government and the Cities,* p. 44.

38. Quoted in the Advisory Committee's *Report,* p. 27.

39. Franz L. Neumann, "Federalism and Freedom," in Arthur W. MacMahon, *Federalism Mature and Emergent* (New York: Russell and Russell, 1962), p. 49.

40. Machiavelli, *The Prince and Other Works,* Alan H. Gilbert, trans. (New York: Hendrick's House, 1946), pp. 99–100.

41. Reinhold Niebuhr, *Moral Man and Immoral Society* (New York: Charles Scribner's Sons, 1932), p. 4.

CHAPTER 8: REFLECTIONS

1. Plato, *Phaedo* in *The Dialogues of Plato,* Jowett trans. (New York: Random House, 1937), p. 483.

2. Samuel P. Huntington, "Conservatism as an Ideology," *American Political Science Review* (June 1957), p. 463.

3. Mulford, *The Nation*, p. 323.

4. *Ibid.*, p. 327.

5. *Ibid.*, p. 324.

6. John W. Burgess, *Political Science and Comparative Constitutional Law* (Boston: Ginn and Co., 1896), II, 6.

7. John Stuart Mill, *Representative Government,* quoted in Arthur W. MacMahon, ed., *Federalism Mature and Emergent* (New York: Russell and Russell, 1962), p. 51.

8. York Willbern, "Losing the Human Touch," *National Municipal Review* (October 1950), p. 444.

9. *The Federalist,* No. 10. In No. 57, Madison wrote: "The aim of every political constitution is, or ought to be, first to obtain for rulers men who possess most wisdom to discern, and most virtue to pursue, the common good of the society."

10. Edmund Burke, *Works* (London: Henry G. Bohn, 1854), I, 446–447.

11. *Ibid.*, II, p. 138.

12. George Sidney Camp, *Democracy* (New York: Harper and Brothers, 1841), p. 212.

13. *Ibid.*, p. 214.

14. *Ibid.*, p. 97.

15. *Ibid.*, pp. 52, 40–42.

16. Lieber, *Manual of Political Ethics,* II, 324–326.

17. *Ibid.*, p. 329.

18. *Ibid.*, pp. 330, 331–332.

19. *Ibid.*, p. 327. It will be seen that the emphases of Francis Lieber are shared by Gulick, Martin, Wood, and Ylvisaker—the proponents of the concept of political virtue presented above.

20. Mulford, *The Nation,* p. 249.

21. *Ibid.*, pp. 240–241.

22. Burgess, *Political Science and Comparative Constitutional Law,* II, 2.

23. *Ibid.*, pp. 50–51.

24. Walter Lippmann, *The Public Philosophy* (Boston: Little, Brown, 1955), pp. 51–52.

25. J. William Fulbright, "Is Government by the People Possible?" in *The Elite and the Electorate* (Santa Barbara: Center for the Study of Democratic Institutions, 1962), p. 5. The Senator quotes from Burke's first speech to his Bristol constituents.

Index